TREKKING IN AUSTRIA'S HOHE TAUERN

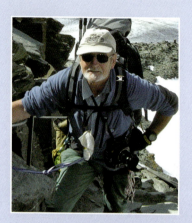

About the Author

Allan has been passionate about mountains and photography since his early teens. He has climbed extensively throughout the Alps, discovering Austria by chance during the early 1970s while trying to avoid atrocious weather conditions in the higher mountains of the Western Alps. Allan maintains that Austria and the Dolomites of neighbouring Italy remain one of mountaineering's best kept secrets with their heady mix of superb scenery, good huts and excellent food and are better suited to the average mountaineer than the higher mountains to the west.

In addition to Austria and the Alps, Allan has climbed from East Africa to the Falkland Islands, the Greater Ranges of Nepal and Pakistan, the lesser known Zagros Mountains of Iran and the Al Hajr Mountains of the Arabian Peninsula.

Not surprisingly Allan is a long-term member of the Austrian Alpine Club, *Sektion Britannia*. Allan is also a member of the Outdoor Writers and Photographers Guild, an Associate of the Royal Photographic Society and a holder of the International Mountain Leader Award. His home is on the edge of the Yorkshire Dales. For more about Allan see **www.allanhartley.co.uk**.

Other Cicerone titles by the author
Trekking in the Stubai Alps
Trekking in the Zillertal Alps

TREKKING IN AUSTRIA'S HOHE TAUERN
THE REICHEN, VENEDIGER AND GROSS GLOCKNER GROUPS

by

Allan Hartley

2 POLICE SQUARE, MILNTHORPE, CUMBRIA LA7 7PY
www.cicerone.co.uk

© Allan Hartley 2010
First edition 2010
ISBN 978 1 85284 568 1

Printed by MCC Graphics, Spain

A catalogue record for this book is available from the British Library.
All photographs are by the author unless otherwise stated.

To Joseph and Lara

Acknowledgements

A special thank you goes to those members of the Austrian Alpine Club who accompanied me while I was compiling this guidebook: Robert Hampson, Ellie Haworth, Barry Walton, Ged O'Neill, Mike Garrett, Peter Jobson, Ros Adams, Marilyn Hartley, Brian Cooper, Stuart Pike, Chris Playford, David Hoad, Donald Weighton, Peter Rogerson, Chris Holmes (Germany), Len Reilly, American nationals David Wrinn and Gerry Becker and last but not least evergreen New Zealander Doug Ball. I also need to acknowledge the specialist skills of Zoe Macdonald for her help translating various German texts and Stuart Pike for his help with all things digital and computing.

Advice to Readers

Readers are advised that, while every effort is made by our authors to ensure the accuracy of guidebooks as they go to print, changes can occur during the lifetime of an edition. Please check the Cicerone website (www.cicerone.co.uk) for any updates before planning your trip. It is also advisable to check information on such things as transport, accommodation and shops locally. Even rights of way can be altered over time. We are always grateful for information about any discrepancies between a guidebook and the facts on the ground, sent by email to info@cicerone.co.uk or by post to Cicerone, 2 Police Square, Milnthorpe LA7 7PY, UK.

Front cover: Donald Weighton and Peter Rogerson enjoy fabulous views from the Kempsen Kopf 3090m (Glockner Rucksack Route, Stage 6)

CONTENTS

INTRODUCTION 11
When to Go 12
Getting There (and Back) 12
Places to Stay 15
Visiting Innsbruck 17
Tourist Offices 19
Post Offices 19
Places to Leave Luggage 19
Health and Fitness 20
Emergencies, Mountain Rescue and Insurance 21
The Austrian Alpine Club 23
About Huts 23
Using this Guide 29
Maps and Guidebooks 32
Alpine Walking Skills 33
Kit List 39
Mountain Guides 41

THE REICHEN GROUP 42
Introduction and Topography 43
The Reichen Group Hut-to-Hut Rucksack Route 46
Stage 1   Mayrhofen to Plauener Hut 47
           Excursions from Plauener Hut 49
Stage 2   Plauener Hut to Birnlucken Hut 53
Stage 3   Birnlucken Hut to Warnsdorfer Hut 59
Stage 4   Warnsdorfer Hut to Krimmler Tauern Haus 61
Stage 5   Krimmler Tauern Haus to Zittauer Hut 62
Stage 6   Zittauer Hut to Richter Hut 65
Stage 7A   Richter Hut to Plauener Hut via the Zillerplatten Scharte ... 67
Stage 7B   Richter Hut to Plauener Hut via the Gams Scharte 71

THE VENEDIGER GROUP 74
Introduction and Topography 75
The Venediger Group Hut-to-Hut Rucksack Route 79
Stage 1   Matrei in Ost Tyrol to Essener Rostocker Hut 80
Stage 2   Essener Rostocker Hut to Johannis Hut via the Turmljoch .. 82

Stage 3	Johannis Hut to the Bonn Matreier Hut via the Zopat Scharte and Eissee Hut.	85
Stage 4	Bonn Matreier Hut to Badener Hut via the Galten Scharte	88
Stage 5	Badener Hut to Neue Prager Hut via the Loebbentorl	94
	Excursion from Neuer Prager Hut	98
Stage 5A	Badener Hut to Venediger Haus (alternative bad weather route)	99
Stage 6	Neue Prager Hut to Sankt Poltener Hut	101
Stage 7	Sankt Poltener Hut to Matreier Tauern Haus	104

The Venediger Glacier Tour 105
Stage 1	Mayrhofen to Warnsdorfer Hut	106
Stage 2	Warnsdorfer Hut to Essener Rostocker Hut via the Gams Spitzl and Mauertorl	107
	Excursions from the Essener Rostocker Hut	110
Stages 3–6	*See Venediger Rucksack Route stages 2–5*	
Stage 7	Neue Prager Hut to Kursinger Hut via the Gross Venediger	116
	Excursion from Kursinger Hut	121
Stage 8	Kursinger Hut to Warnsdorfer Hut via the Obersulzbach Kees glacier and Gams Spitzl	122

THE GROSS GLOCKNER GROUP 128

Introduction and Topography 129

The Glockner Group Hut-to-Hut Rucksack Route 132
Stage 1	Lucknerhaus to Studl Hut	135
	Excursions from the Studl Hut	138
Stage 2	Studl Hut to Salm Hut via the Pfort Scharte	151
Stage 3	Salm Hut to Glockner Haus	153
Stage 4	Glockner Haus to Fusch via the Phandl Scharte	156
Stage 5	Fusch to Gleiwitzer Hut	161
Stage 6	Gleiwitzer Hut to Heinrich Schwaiger Haus	162
	Excursions from Heinrich Schwaiger Haus	168
Stage 6A	Gleiwitzer Hut to Kaprun	171
Stage 7	Heinrich Schwaiger to Rudolfs Hut/Berg Hotel	172
	Excursions from Rudolfs Hut	175
Stage 8	Rudolfs Hut to Sudetendeutsche Hut via the Kalser Tauern and Gradetz Sattel	181
	Excursion from the Sudetendeutsche Hut	187
Stage 8A	Rudolfs Hut to Kalser Tauern Haus	189
Stage 9	Sudetendeutsche Hut to Matrei in Ost Tyrol	190

HUT DIRECTORY 192

APPENDIX A Useful Contacts 236
APPENDIX B German–English Glossary 237
APPENDIX C Further Reading 240
APPENDIX D Across the Hohe Tauern National Park 241

Index 244

Mountain warning

Mountain walking can be a dangerous activity carrying a risk of personal injury or death. It should be undertaken only by those with a full understanding of the risks and with the training and experience to evaluate them. While every care and effort has been taken in the preparation of this guide, the user should be aware that conditions can be highly variable and can change quickly, materially affecting the seriousness of a mountain walk. Therefore, except for any liability which cannot be excluded by law, neither Cicerone nor the author accept liability for damage of any nature (including damage to property, personal injury or death) arising directly or indirectly from the information in this book.

To call out the Mountain Rescue, ring 140 or the international emergency number 112: this will connect you via any available network. Once connected to the emergency operator, ask for the police.

Negotiating car sized boulders above the Eissee (Reichen Group Stage 7)

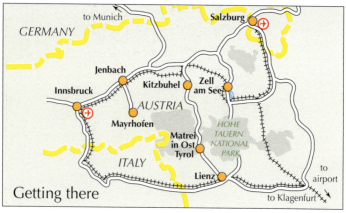

Getting there

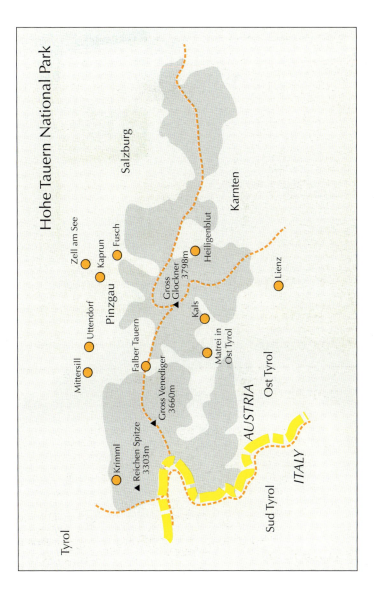

Looking back from the Gross Glockner across the Klein Glockner toward Erzherzog Johann Hut (Glockner Rucksack Route, Stage 1 Excursion)

INTRODUCTION

On the Sonnblick Kees glacier (Glockner Rucksack Route, Stage 7 Excursion)

The Hohe Tauern National Park is the largest national park not only in Austria and the Eastern Alps but the whole of continental Europe, comprising an area of 1800km². Within Austria it embraces the provinces of Tyrol, Salzburg and Karnten (Carinthia). Not surprisingly the national park's main point of focus is the Gross Glockner, the highest mountain in Austria, closely followed by the Gross Venediger, the fourth highest mountain and one which also has the distinction of having the highest number of connected glaciers in Austria. To the west, the Hohe Tauern merges with the Reichen Group to encompass the largest concentration of 3000m peaks in the Eastern Alps. The Hohe Tauern National Park is now a World Heritage Area, ranking alongside Yosemite, Serengeti, the Galapagos Islands and Mount Everest.

To the north of the National Park is the Pinzgau valley where, from the towns of Kitzbuhel, Mittersill and Zell am See, there are easy transport routes to the south to Matrei in Ost Tyrol for the Virgental and Venediger Group and Kals for the Gross Glockner.

This guidebook concentrates on three areas – the Reichen, Venediger and Gross Glockner Groups. In each section, descriptions are provided for various hut-to-hut tours along with excursions and recommended climbs. Like my other Alpine trekking guides, this guide has been written to offer walkers as much flexibility as possible, describing all the options that occur as you tour from hut to hut. For example there are the familiar Rucksack Routes and Glacier Tours, routes that are linear and routes that are circular. There is also the option to walk from Mayrhofen, through the Reichen Group and across the Venediger to end with a climb on the Gross Glockner, all within the span of a two-week holiday (see Appendix D, Across the Hohe Tauern).

The Hohe Tauern provides opportunities for all mountain enthusiasts, whatever their aspirations. It is ideal for first-time visitors to the Alps, particularly family groups with adventurous children, but it is even more so for aspiring alpinists, who are wrong to see the Hohe Tauern as tame. These mountains can challenge even the most experienced. You will not be disappointed.

Gruss Gott und gut Bergtouren!

WHEN TO GO

The summer season usually starts in mid-June and ends in late September. June is not the best time to visit as it is not unusual to come across large quantities of old snow which will be left lying on the north-facing slopes, in places such as the Rainbach Scharte, Zopat Scharte and Loebbentorl.

July weather will be warmer and will see the winter snow recede further. There will be more people in the mountains and at the huts. August is the peak season, when most Europeans take their holidays and the huts will be at their busiest then. The weather is also at its most settled but it is not unusual to see cloud build up in the late mornings and thunderstorms arrive in the evenings. August is also the month when most of the villages in the Hohe Tauern hold their summer church festivals, known as *kirchtags*. They are worth a visit, good fun and enjoyed by all. In September with the arrival of autumn the huts will be quieter and the weather cooler.

The author's personal choice for a two-week holiday is either the middle of July or the first two weeks in September.

GETTING THERE (AND BACK)

Getting to Austria is relatively straightforward no matter how you decide to travel. For the purposes of these treks, you will probably arrive in Austria in the medieval city of **Innsbruck**, the provincial capital of the Tyrol. Transport to the starting points for tours in the Reichen Group, Venediger and Gross Glockner is described from Innsbruck within each section.

By Air

Even if you travel by air, which is without doubt the quickest way to get to Austria, you do not always have

GETTING THERE (AND BACK)

sufficient time to leave the UK in the morning, fly to Austria, catch a train to Innsbruck, Jenbach–Mayrhofen, Kitzbuhel then Zell am See, and then make your way to one of the huts before nightfall. At best you should plan to stay overnight in Innsbruck and then continue your journey the day after. However if your plan is to tour in the Reichen Group, it is just about possible to get to the Plauener Hut by early evening if you do not have any hold-ups!

Both British Airways and Lufthansa run several flights a day from London and Manchester. Other budget carriers also operate services from Luton, Stansted and Gatwick. (See Appendix A for airline websites.)

Travelling by air gets you to mainland Europe quickly but then you may loose precious time transferring to the railway station (*Hauptbahnhof*) and may experience frustrating delays and hold-ups just finding your way about.

At **Munich,** the airport connects direct with the regional railway network where there are frequent trains every 20mins or so. Follow the train signs DB and S. The set-up is similar to the London Underground, which means you need a pre-paid ticket before getting on the train. Do not push your luck without a ticket, as the Germans do not take kindly to freeloaders, no matter where you come from. There is also a booking office in the arrivals hall adjacent to the concession counters for car hire, hotel reservations and so on. This facility is not always open but if it is get your

A party crossing the Obersulzbach Kees glacier with Gross Venediger in the background (Venediger Glacier Tour, Stage 8)

ticket to Innsbruck *hin und zuruck* (return). There are express trains every two hours or so. Once on your journey you need to get off the regional train at *Munchen Ost* (Munich East) and change platforms to get on one of the intercity trains (*schnell zug*). Lookout for the sign boards on the side of the train and get on the first one that has Innsbruck or Brennero, Venezia, Venedig on it: anything heading into Italy or Switzerland will do, as they all have to go via Innsbruck.

If the ticket office at Munich airport is closed you can get your ticket at Munich East ticket office, which you will find at road level with other shops and fast food outlets. With express trains it is also possible to pay on the train, sometimes at a premium, if you can show that you had to rush and didn't have enough time to get to the ticket office.

At **Salzburg,** take the 'Line 2' bus service from the airport to the *Hauptbahnhof* (railway station), from where a rail ticket to Innsbruck can be purchased.

If you are planning to tour the Reichen Group there is no need to go to Innsbruck. Take the train as far as Jenbach then transfer to the Zillertalbahn narrow-gauge railway for the 30-mile, one-hour train ride up the Zillertal valley to Mayrhofen. The overall journey time is about two hours depending on connections. The last train to Mayrhofen from Jenbach is at 18:22hr.

If your plan is to climb in the Glockner region, again there is no need to go to Innsbruck. Take the train to Zell am See or Kitzbuhel, then use the local bus services.

At Innsbruck airport, there is a bus service plus taxis to get you to the city centre and the Hauptbahnhof; then use regional trains to wherever you plan to tour.

By Rail

Consult with National Rail Enquiries or Eurostar, but these are the two most commonly used routes. (Each will get you to Innsbruck within 18 hours.)

- London/Dover/Calais/Paris/Zurich/Innsbruck
- London/Dover/Ostend/Brussels/Munich/Innsbruck

See these websites for further details:
- DB: Deutsche Bundesbahn (German Railways) www.reiseauskunft.bahn.de
- OBB: Osterreichische Bundesbahnen (Austrian Railways) www.oebb.at
- Postbus: www.postbus.at

By Road

The most direct route is via the Dover–Ostend channel crossing, then making use of the motorway system to Munich and into Austria at Kufstein, followed by the short drive up the Inn valley to Innsbruck. Whatever your chosen route consult your motoring organisation before setting out. If there is more than one driver it is possible to get to Innsbruck in 10–12 hours from Calais or Ostend.

PLACES TO STAY

It is also important when parking your car to remember to consider getting back to it, which is not always easy when you drop down into another valley. It is best to leave your car at one of the major towns with good railway connections to Innsbruck, Jenbach or Zell am See, if possible.

The Return Journey
For those travelling by air, the last day of your vacation needs to be devoted to making the journey home. See the individual sections for descriptions.

Journey time from Innsbruck to Munich airport is around 2–2½hrs, to Salzburg 2hrs. From Innsbruck the trains to Munich leave at:

- 08:38/10:38/12:37/14:37/16:37/18:37/20:37hrs.

From Innsbruck the trains to Salzburg are roughly every two hours:

- 09:30/11:30/13:30hrs.

From Mayrhofen the first train to Jenbach is at 05:52hrs, thereafter every hour from 06:40hrs onwards. The first train from Jenbach to Munich is at 10:38hrs, and to Salzburg at 09:50hrs. Remember to change trains at Munich East and get on the regional shuttle service train S8 marked *Flughafen*.

See Appendix B for some useful German words and phrases to use when travelling.

PLACES TO STAY

There is no shortage of good places to stay throughout Austria as the whole country is geared to tourism and catering for visitors.

Hotels
Hotels in Innsbruck will be more expensive than hotels and guesthouses in the surrounding local villages. If you are not bothered about nightlife then you will find good bargains in the towns of Mayrhofen, Kitzbuhel, Matrei, Kaprun and Zell am See.

In Innsbruck, hotels can be booked from the tourist information centre at the railway station. Some recommended places are listed below.

In Innsbruck
Alt Pradl Hotel Located 10mins walk from the railway station and 20mins from the old town. Quiet.

- tel 0043 (0) 5123 45156
- email info@hotel-altpradl.at
- website www.hotel-altpradl.at

Weisses Kreuz (The White Cross) A touch of the old, medieval Innsbruck, located in the heart of the old town, its claim to fame is that Mozart stayed here when in Innsbruck to play for the Royal Court at the Hofburg Palace.

- tel 0043 (0) 5125 94790
- email hotel@weisseskreuz.at
- website www.weisseskreuz.at

The Goldene Krone (The Golden Crown) Located on Maria Theresien Strasse near the Triumphal Arch.

Trekking in Austria's Hohe Tauern

- tel 0043 (0) 5125 86160
- email info@goldene-krone.at
- website www.goldene-krone.at

Nepomuk's Backpackers' Hostel Located just off the main square in the old part of the Alte Stadt.

- tel 0043 (0) 6647 879197 or
  0043 (0) 5125 84118
- email mail@nepomuks.at
- website www.nepomuks.at

In Mayrhofen
Hotel Siegelerhof Opposite the tourist information office, 5mins walk from the railway station. The hotel is managed by the Hausberger family who provide good inexpensive bed and breakfast accommodation. You can also leave surplus bags there to pick up on your return.

- tel 0043 (0) 5285 62493 or 62424
- email info@ hotel-siegelerhof.at
- website www.hotel-siegelerhof.at

In Matrei in Ost Tyrol
Hotels may be reserved at the tourist information office in the village square.

The Sport Hotel Located just off the main road opposite the bus station at the entrance to the Virgental valley and gateway to the Venediger.

- tel 0043 (0) 4875 20104
- email riepler.alois@utanet
- website www.jugend-und-sporthotel.at

In Salzburg
Zur Post Hotel 5mins from the airport and 15mins from the fine old city centre.

- tel 0043 (0) 6628 32339
- email hotelzurpost@EUnet.at
- website www.hotelzurpost.info

Campsites

For those travelling by road and wishing to camp, there are good campsites throughout the region: in the Zillertal valley at Schlitters, Kaltenbach, Zell am Ziller; at Laubichl on the outskirts of Mayrhofen; at Matrei in Ost Tyrol, 300m to the south on the Huben road; and also at Pragraten in the Virgental valley. Groups intending to camp should enquire from the campsite warden about reduced fees while they are away. This is referred to as *leeres zelt*.

VISITING INNSBRUCK

Innsbruck is the capital city of the province of Tyrol, named after the river on which it stands. It is overlooked by the Karwendel group of mountains, and was made famous as a venue for the Winter Olympics Sports. The city is well worth a visit in its own right, having the right mix of city life and cultural history but with the mountains not far away.

See the map overleaf for locations of

- railway and bus stations
- tourist information and post offices
- main historical sites
- the Alpine Museum
- Hotels

OeAV Museum

Should you have time on your hands the Alpine (OeAV) Museum in Innsbruck is worthy of a visit. Located within the Hofburg Imperial Palace in the Old Town, it has many fine exhibits

Innsbruck's mediaeval Alte Stadt with the Golden Roof, Stadt Turm tower and Karwendal mountains

Trekking in Austria's Hohe Tauern

Central Innsbruck

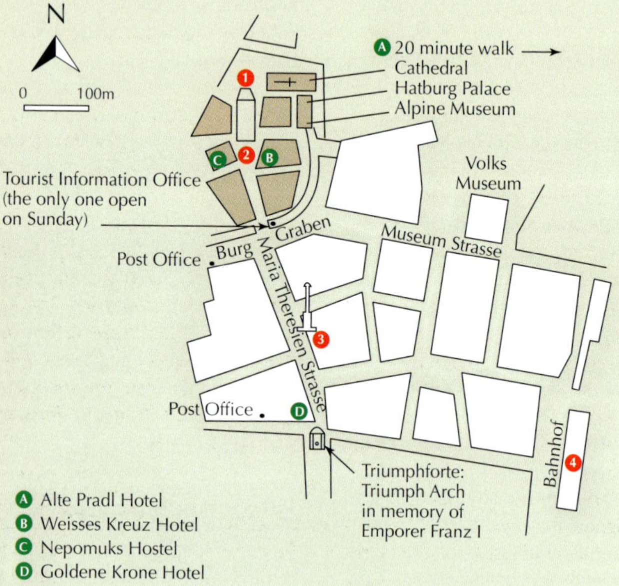

N

0   100m

Ⓐ 20 minute walk →
Cathedral
Hatburg Palace
Alpine Museum

Volks Museum

Tourist Information Office
(the only one open on Sunday)

Post Office

Burg Graben

Maria Theresien Strasse

Museum Strasse

Post Office

Bahnhof

Triumphforte:
Triumph Arch
in memory of
Emporer Franz I

Ⓐ Alte Pradl Hotel
Ⓑ Weisses Kreuz Hotel
Ⓒ Nepomuks Hostel
Ⓓ Goldene Krone Hotel

❶ Goldenes Dachl: The Golden Roof. Ornate royal box built by Emporer Maximillian I in 1500. The roof is covered in gold-plated tiles.

❷ Old part of the city and town square that contains many fine examples of architectural styles and includes the Imperial Palace (*Hofburg*) and City Tower (*stadtturm*).

❸ Statue of Annasaule: St Anna's column erected in 1706 in thanksgiving for the successful defence against the Bavarian invasion during the war of Spanish succession.

❹ Hauptbahnhof: railway and bus station, airport bus terminus, information centre and taxi service.

from alpinism's golden era, perhaps the most notable being memorabilia of Hermann Buhl's solo ascent of Nanga Parbat in the Pakistani Karakoram.

The museum is open Monday to Saturday during normal business hours.

TOURIST OFFICES

In Innsbruck at the main railway station (Hauptbahnhof) there is a tourist information office on the lower level opposite the ticket booking hall. There is another at the entrance to the Old Town Square (*Alte Statd*) on Museum Strasse at the road junction of Burg Graben and Maria Therasien Strasse. This bureau is the only one in Innsbruck that is open on Sunday, and has a money exchange facility.

In Mayrhofen, the main tourist information office, the *Europahaus*, is located five minutes' walk from the railway station, on Durster Strasse. There are other satellite offices located throughout the town.

In Matrei in Ost Tyrol, the tourist office is located in the village square adjacent to the post office.

General enquiries about visiting Austria in advance of your trip should be addressed to the Austrian National Tourist Office (see Appendix A, Useful Contacts).

POST OFFICES

Post offices are open Monday to Friday 08:00hrs to12:00hrs, then 14:00hrs to 18:00hrs. They have fax facilities and a foreign currency exchange service.

Innsbruck's post office is located on the Mark Stainer Strasse near the entrance to the Alte Stadt, and on Maxillian Strasse near the Triumphal Arch.

Mayrhofen's post office is located on the Pfarrer Krapf Strasse just off the main street through the town.

Matrei in Ost Tyrol's post office is located next to the tourist information centre in the main square.

Post between Austria and the UK usually takes about five days. All the mountain huts sell postcards which can be purchased and mailed from their own postboxes. The mail is then taken down the valley, usually once a week, and deposited at the main post office. This means that post to the UK *from the huts* will take 10 to 14 days.

PLACES TO LEAVE LUGGAGE

There are luggage facilities at all the bus and railway stations. However for security reasons there may be restrictions on using the luggage lockers for longer than 48 hours. Leave a note with your belongings stating who you are, your passport number, where you are going, your mobile telephone number and details of when you will be back.

Alternatively, if you are staying at one of the hotels, most hoteliers are quite happy to store luggage until you return.

A group of well-equipped young teenagers

HEALTH AND FITNESS

Taking children

I have been asked many times about the suitability of hut-to-hut touring for children.

Most children I know or have met love visiting the various huts and the sense of freedom it brings. The Austrian Alpine Club also actively encourages children to participate in mountain activities.

My own daughter traversed the entire length of the Venediger Rucksack Route and undertook the rigours of the Glacier Tour climbing several peaks along the way when she was 15 years old. If children are capable of ascending Ben Nevis,

Snowdon or doing the round of Helvellyn then they will surely enjoy some of these tours. But only parents can decide, since some of the days' outings are quite long. Children need to be fit, happy to be in the mountains for long periods at a time and easily entertained by reading books, playing Scrabble or simply chatting. The best thing, however, is to have a few friends with them for company.

Fitness
You do not have to be super-fit to undertake these tours but it is essential that you are comfortable walking for six hours continuously while carrying a rucksack weighing in the region of 12 to 15kg.

Coping with altitude
The average altitude of the tour(s) is in the region of 2500m to 3000m (8000 to 10,000ft). It is therefore not normal for people visiting the Hohe Tauern to suffer badly from altitude sickness. However that is not to say you will not feel the effects of altitude, such as feeling out of puff, a mild headache and slowed pace, particularly on the high peaks of the Gross Venediger and Gross Glockner.

The best defence against altitude is to be as fit as possible, to eat and drink normally and to get adequate sleep.

European Health Insurance Card (EHIC)
This card, previously known as the E111, is available free from any post office: all you have to do is fill in the form to receive a credit card sized EHIC identity card that will entitle you to free medical care in any EU member state. Should you be unfortunate enough to need medical attention while on holiday then this card will help. However the EHIC only entitles you to those services provided free in the member state. It does not cover any aspect of medical repatriation.

The top and bottom line with the EHIC is that you will still need to be insured.

EMERGENCIES, MOUNTAIN RESCUE AND INSURANCE

All the routes described in this book involve sustained activity in a mountain environment. Inevitably this increases the risk of an accident taking place. This means that a severe fall, breaking a limb or some other serious mishap will result in the mountain rescue team being called out.

As noted elsewhere one of the benefits of membership of the OeAV (Austrian Alpine Club) is mountain rescue insurance in case of accident. This can be supplemented from a specialist insurance company; details of some of these are available from the Austrian Alpine Club UK section or by simply scanning the adverts in one of the many climbing magazines. Similarly the British Mountaineering Council, the BMC, has an excellent insurance policy, which is available to non-members.

The value of insurance should not be underestimated as the cost of a mountain rescue can be considerable when helicopters, police and professional mountain guides are brought into use. Unlike in the UK, where mountain rescue services are generally provided free, in the Alps most countries will charge the hapless victim. Be warned!

Mountain rescue is as much about prevention as it is about cure so please practise your glacier travel before you go. Check out all your gear and practise the time-consuming tasks of putting on crampons/harnesses/

EMERGENCY TELEPHONE NUMBERS IN AUSTRIA

It is worth remembering that emergency services operate on a different satellite frequency and that the following numbers can be dialled from a mobile telephone even when the phone indicates there is no reception from your service provider. Fortunately in Austria mobile telephone reception is excellent.

- Mountain Rescue (Bergrettung) 140
- Red Cross (Rotes Kreutz) 144
- European emergency telephone number 112

Alpine Distress Signal
Help required: signalled by shouting, whistling or flashing a torch 6 times at 10 second intervals. Then a pause for one minute then repeat.

Answer received: signalled by shouting, whistle or flashing a torch at 20 second intervals. Then a pause for one minute then repeat.

Signals to Helicopters
Help required: arms outstretched, feet together to give a bold Y outline as in YES, help is required.

All is well: one arm raised above the head, one arm lowered to give an N outline as in NO, help not required.

roping up; and then practise your crevasse rescue techniques. Basic though this may seem I am still amazed how often we forget to do this and how often we get it wrong.

THE AUSTRIAN ALPINE CLUB

Founded in 1862, huts throughout the Hohe Tauern are administered by the Austrian Alpine Club (Oesterreichischer Alpenverein, OeAV), founded in 1862, or by the German Alpine Club (DAV), except for those that are private or belong to the Oesterreichischer Touristen Klub (the OeTK) and those in the South Tyrol which are owned and administered by the Italian Alpine Club (CAI).

Membership of the Austrian Alpine Club is open to all regardless of ability and is recommended because of the reduced hut rates and the provision of mountain rescue insurance that comes with it.

The United Kingdom section of the OeAV was formed in 1948, just after World War II, to foster Austro-Anglo relationships between like-minded people in the spirit of mountaineering and to make membership easier for British mountaineers.

Presently the Club has over 6000 UK members. Current annual membership rates are £38 for adults, £66.50 for a husband and wife or family group, £28.50 for seniors and juveniles. On acceptance of membership, the Club provides an excellent Members' Handbook packed with useful information.

The Club's principal activities include development and provision of mountain huts, marking and maintenance of footpaths, the production of maps and guidebooks and the organising of mountaineering courses and expeditions. In addition the Club is becoming increasingly involved in environmental issues, particularly activities that are seen to spoil the mountains by either physical or visual pollution.

The Austrian Alpine Club enjoys full reciprocal rights agreements with the alpine clubs of France (CAF), Switzerland (CAS), Italy (CAI) and Germany (DAV). This means that while in the Reichen group, should you cross into the South Tyrol to stay at the Birnlucken Hut you will pay the same fees as those enjoyed by members of the Italian Alpine Club, and vice versa.

The Austrian Alpine Club also has a thriving UK Section which has an active indoor and outdoor meets programme to suit most members and publishes a quarterly newsletter (see www.aacuk.org.uk and Appendix A for full contact information).

ABOUT HUTS

The word 'hut' is a misnomer as all the huts in the Hohe Tauern as described here are more akin to mountain inns or guest houses, and provide simple overnight accommodation in the form of rooms or dormitories together with some form of restaurant service (see

'Meals and Menus' below). This means that if you are travelling through the mountains you do not have to return to the valley to stock up on provisions every few days.

On arrival at a hut it is essential that you make contact with the hut guardian (the *huttenwirt*). Normally this is a husband and wife team, with the husband sometimes being a mountain guide (*Bergfuehrer*).

The huttenwirt will normally be found near the kitchen (*kuche* or at the hut office (*bureau*, *buro*). You should greet this person by saying *'Gruss Gott'* and presenting your passport and OeAV membership card. You should then explain that you are member of the Austrian Alpine Club *Sektion Britannia* and that you would like some accommodation.

If you do not speak German and feel uncomfortable with asking for rooms in German, then write down the phrase noted in the language section. Be polite by asking *bitte* (please) when handing over the message and answering *danke* (thank you) when the message is returned. Trivial as this may seem these polite gestures are extremely important and will go a long way to ensure a pleasant stay.

Having made your reservation for a bed (*bett*) or dormitory (*matratzenlager*) you should stow your boots in the boot rack and hang your other clobber – rope, axe, crampons – on the pegs provided in the hallway or *schuraum*.

If you are wet on arrival, your waterproofs should be shaken as dry as possible outside the hut and hung up with your other tackle. If you are in a group do not mill around the doorways and again if you are wet make sure you leave as much surplus water and dirt off your boots outside the hut. Many of the huts are spotlessly clean and for the benefits of all guests should be allowed to remain that way.

The OeAV does not provide visitors with hut shoes, so you need to take your own to wander around the hut in as boots upstairs are strictly forbidden (*verboten*).

Should the hut be full you may have to take residence in the *winterraum*, which is usually reserved for ski mountaineers and those visiting when the hut is closed. Most huts in the Hohe Tauern are open from early June to the end of September. The winterraum is generally an annexe to the hut and may double as a storeroom or shelter for animals, as at the Kursinger Hut. While the winterraum can be quite cosy remember to keep your gear off the floor, as it is usually the home of more permanent four-pawed residents.

Should the hut be beyond full you will be provided with a mattress for *notlager* which, roughly translated, means 'sleeping with the furniture', be it on the floor, in the corridors, on tables, on benches or simply anywhere you can lie down.

Only on very rare occasions will you be asked to move on by the

About Huts

View from the Warnsdorfer Hut – the Birnlucken Pass (2667m) is the obvious gap on the left skyline and the Reichen Spitze the dominant peak on the right (Reichen Rucksack Route, Stage 3)

huttenwirt but only when bed space has been secured at an adjacent hut and only when there is sufficient daylight for you to reach your destination. In the Hohe Tauern all of this is an unusual scenario, and can lead to some cosy if somewhat noisy situations.

At the hut you will also require a sheet sleeping bag (*schlafsack*) for use with the blankets and bedding which the hut provides. This is to minimise the amount of washing required and reduce water pollution. This is a compulsory requirement and if you do not have one the huttenwirt will rent you one.

Elsewhere in the hut you will find male and female washrooms and toilets. Most of these facilities in the Hohe Tauern are good but a number are at best described as basic but adequate. Most huts also have a drying room, or *trockenraum*, which you should find close to the front door. Likewise most huts have a small shop where visitors can purchase basic provisions such as chocolate, biscuits and cakes.

Thereafter the heart and soul of the hut is the *gaste stube* or dining room. Here you will find all manner of activities going on from groups planning their next day, people celebrating a climb or a birthday or people just chatting. The atmosphere is best described by the German word *gemutlichkeit* which means homely or friendly and is something that is fostered and cherished throughout the whole of Austria.

At the end of your stay you should remember to make your bed and fold your blankets, to look around to make sure you've left nothing behind and to search out the huttenwirt and thank them for a pleasant stay. You should then fill in the hut book to record your stay and to indicate where you are going next.

The cost of accommodation is published annually and available on the Austrian Alpine Club website – www.alpenverein.at. Click on the Hütten/Wege link and choose Tarifordnung. (At the time of going to press dormitory accommodation in a Category I hut was €10 and in a Category III hut €16.)

Reservations

For small groups of three or four people it is not necessary to make a reservation at many of the huts. However, if you are a group of six or more, it is strongly recommended that you make contact with the hut using the address provided in the hut directory at the back of this guidebook, and sending a prepaid stamped addressed envelope, before you go. It is also essential to book if you intend to climb the Gross Glockner and Gross Venediger as these huts are always busy.

Most of the huts in the Hohe Tauern now have websites and email addresses, which makes it easier than ever to get in touch with the hut to make reservations. Again, see the Hut Directory for details.

It is worth noting that members are only allowed three consecutive nights at any one hut, although this is not strictly enforced.

Meals and Menus

All huts have some sort of restaurant service to cover the three daily meals: breakfast (*fruehstuck*), lunch (*mittagessen*) and dinner (*abendessen*).

Breakfast is served from about 06:00hrs to approximately 07:30hrs. Thereafter no meals are available until lunchtime as the hut staff are busy with general housekeeping. Breakfast is seen as the worst value for money but unless you are carrying your own provisions you will have little choice other than to accept it.

Lunchtime usually takes place from 12:00hrs to 14:00hrs but varies depending on the hut. It is also possible to purchase simple meals like soup, *kase brot* and *apfelstrudl* at most of the huts throughout the afternoon.

Dinner is the main meal of the day and is generally served from 18:00hrs to 19:30hrs. Apart from meals listed on the menu, *bergsteigeressen* will be available along with other meals. Literally translated the word means 'mountain climbers' food' and in reality that is what it is, even if it is pot luck what you get! However it is a

About Huts

Comfortable accommodation at the Sankt Poltener Hut – note the mountain rescue donations tin on the table (Venediger Rucksack Route, Stage 6)

low-priced meal and must contain a minimum of 500 calories. The meal generally comprises spaghetti or pasta, potatoes, some meat or sausage, sometimes a fried egg or maybe a dumpling. There is no hard and fast rule other than that it is relatively inexpensive and that there is usually a lot of it!

Generally the procedure for ordering meals is that you first organise a table. There is no formality, but sometimes, when mountaineering training courses are being run, groups of tables may be marked private or reserved (*privat reservierung*). Having sat down one of the waitresses (*frauline*) will take your order. Alternatively, you may have to go to the counter or kitchen (*kuche*) to order, or there may be a sign saying *selbsbedienungs*, which means self-service.

The general rule for paying for food and drink is to pay an accumulative bill. Keep notes of what you eat and drink to aid checking at the time of paying. Bills can become considerable when staying at a hut for more than a couple of nights.

Because of the excellent service the huts provide it is obvious that very little of one's own food needs to be carried. However, you may want to take your own dry rations such as tea, coffee, bread and cheese. This permits you to make your own snacks and by borrowing cups and purchasing *eine litre teewasser* you can brew up for a little cost. The only facility not provided for is self-catering, which does seem a little pointless when all the meals are reasonably priced.

Tea, coffee, hot chocolate, lemonade, beer, wine and schnapps are all available at the huts. Breakfast (*fruehstuck*) is served between 06:00hrs and 07:30hrs and comprises two or three slices of bread, a portion of butter, jam and cheese and tea or coffee. If you don't finish it, take it with you! You pay for it all. Lunch (*mittagessen*) and dinner (*abendessen*) are served with a selection of vegetables or salad and there should be vegetarian (*vegetarische*) options. Drinks are served in quarter (*viertel*) or half (*halb*) litres, or large (*gross*) or small (*klein*), and may be hot (*heiss*) or cold (*kalt*). See the glossary (Appendix B) for some useful words and phrases when reading menus or ordering food and drink.

As a guideline for working out a budget, typical meal price lists can be obtained from the UK Section of the Austrian Alpine Club. (At the time of going to press, their website – www.aacuk.org.uk – was estimating the cost of dinner in a hut at between €7 and €16, depending on what you opt for.) Alternatively a budget cost can be worked out on the basis of prices charged in most British pubs for a decent bar meal plus drinks. (The unit of currency in Austria is the Euro, as in Germany and Italy.)

TYPICAL MENU ITEMS

German	English
Mittag und Abendessen	Lunch and Dinner
Wiener Schnitzel	Breaded veal/pork fillets
Jager Schnitzel	Veal/pork fillets with mushroom topping
Tyroler Grotzl	Fried potato and eggs
Spiegeleier und Schinken	Fried eggs and bacon
Gulash	Cubes of beef in a rich sauce
Zweibelrostbraten	Broiled or fried beef with onions
Wurst Brot	Sausage and bread
Kase Brot	Cheese and bread
Schinken Brot	Ham and bread
Tagesuppe	Soup of the day
Knodelsuppe	Soup with dumplings
Wurstsuppe	Soup with sausages
Kaiserschmarren	Sweet pancakes
Apfelstrudel	Apple pie
Compote	Fresh or tinned fruit
Bergsteigeressen	Climbers' pot-luck meal at low cost

Meals are served with a selection of vegetables or salad:	
German	**English**
Brot/Brotchen	Bread/Bread rolls
Kartoffeln	Potato
Gemuse	Vegetables
Reis	Rice
Salt	Salt
Pfeffer	Pepper
Senf	Mustard
Drinks:	
Heiss/Kalt	Hot/Cold
Gross/Klein	Large/Small
Viertel/Halb	Quarter/Half

USING THIS GUIDE

Paths, Tracks and Waymarks

Paths throughout the Hohe Tauern are waymarked roughly every hundred metres with a daub of red paint.

At intersections, paths frequently have a signpost or alternatively have a red and white paint marker with a designated path number; this in turn is cross-referenced by maps and guidebooks including this one.

Emergency information on a signpost

A Helicopter recognition number
B Telephone number for mountain rescue
C European emergency services
D Grid references
E Altitude

Routes described in this guide, such as on the Reichen Group Runde Tour and the Venediger Hohenweg vary from traditional mountain paths to tracks across boulder fields and rough ground. There is also steep ground, late summer snow and fixed wire ropes here and there to aid stability.

Paths for hut-to-hut routes are frequently marked with a signpost just outside the hut, which will give the standard time in hours for the distance between huts without stops (treat these times with caution: see below).

The tracks onto and across glaciers are not normally marked as the route may vary from year to year. Also if venturing onto glaciers you are expected to have the necessary know-how and route finding skills. However, sometimes the local guides will place marker poles on the glacier to aid route finding, such as on the heavily crevassed Obersulzbach Kees glacier.

Where the route follows a river, stream or glacier and reference is made to the left or right bank, this is when viewed in the direction of flow. So when ascending the left bank will be on your right. To avoid confusion, efforts have been made throughout the text to add a compass bearing to ensure that you go in the right direction!

In general, no great demand will be made on your route-finding skills. If there are any places that require particular care, they will be highlighted in a pale blue box at the end of the description. However route-finding is naturally made much more difficult in mist, rain and snow.

> Please note that routes may change from the published description as a result of landslips, avalanches and erosion.

MOUNTAIN GRADES

Alpine ascents are often given a descriptive mountaineering grade:

- F Facile – easy
- PD Peu Difficile – a little bit difficult
- AD Assez Difficile – quite difficult

Plus or minus signs are often added to these grades to signify that they are at the higher or lower end of the grade respectively.

Technical climbing ascents are also sometimes given a UIAA (International Mountaineering and Climbing Federation) technical grade:

- I British grade of moderate
- II British grade of difficult
- III British grade of very difficult/mild severe

Route descriptions and sketch maps

The routes described follow recognised paths and tracks corresponding to those indicted on maps and signposts.

However, to aid route-finding across unfamiliar ground, each daily tour itinerary is fully described and illustrated with a sketch map indicating the main topographical features that will be observed en route.

Route grading

The route described is for people who are already involved in some sort of mountain activity on a regular basis. It goes without saying that the tours are moderately strenuous and require the ability to carry a full pack for an average of six hours a day. In terms of alpine grading, the majority of the routes fall into the mountaineering grade of easy to moderate, comprising

MOUNTAIN TERMINOLOGY

The following German words may be useful in route-finding and getting about.

German	English
Tal	Valley
Gletscher/Kees	Glacier
Randkluft/Spalten	Bergschrund/Crevasses
Eis	Ice
Bach/Wasserfal	River/Stream/Waterfall
See/Lac	Tarn/Lake
Wald/Baum	Forest/Tree
Alm	Alpine hut/Pasture
Weg	Way/Footpath
Berg	Mountain
Band/Grat/Kamm	Ledge/Ridge
Nadel	Needle/Pinnacle
Gipfel/Spitze	Summit
Wilde/Aperer	Snow peak/Rockpeak
Torl/Scharte/Sattel/Nieder	Col/Saddle/Pass
Kessel/Grube/Kar	Couloir/Basin/Combe
Nord/Sud/Ost/West	North/South/East/West
Links/Rechts/Geradeaus	Left/Right/Straight ahead
Uber/Unter	Over/Under
Hinter/Mittler/Vorder	Further/Middle/Nearer
Inner/Ausser	Inner/Outer
Wanderkarte	Map

MOUNTAIN TERMINOLOGY

German	English
Steinslag	Stone fall
Schweirig/Leicht	Difficult/Easy
Gefahrlich	Dangerous
Alpenvereins	Alpine Club
Bergfuehrer	Mountain Guide
Nur fur geubte	Only for the experienced
Gesprutt	Route is closed/barred
Bergrettung	Mountain Rescue
Kabel/Pickle	Rope/Ice axe

sustained mountain walking, requiring the ability to negotiate steep ground, scramble over rocks, cross late summer snow, make use of fixed wire ropes and have a good head for heights.

Standard times

At the beginning of each route description a **standard time** in hours (*stunden*) is quoted as an estimate of time required from hut to hut. This standard time generally equates to that given in the Austrian Alpine Club's green Hut Book. The standard time stated is for hours spent moving and does not include lunch stops and other breaks. Most British parties find some difficulty in meeting standard times indicated by signposts outside huts. Do not worry. A lot of these standard times are unattainable or seem to have been set by Olympic athletes. With this in mind, the route descriptions in this book give the **actual time** required when carrying a heavy rucksack.

If you undertake any of the tours with children you are advised to add at least one hour to the given time to allow for frequent picnic stops. Similarly, aspirant alpinists should make due allowance to the standard time while they learn the rudiments of glacier travel and the very time-consuming activities of roping up and putting crampons on and taking them off.

MAPS AND GUIDEBOOKS

The following are available from the UK Section of the Austrian Alpine Club.

Maps (*Alpenvereinskarte*)
- Sheet 35/3
  Zillertal Alpen Ost (east)
  Scale 1:25,000

- Sheet 36
  Venediger Group
  Scale 1:25,000

- Sheet 39
  Granat Spitze Group
  Scale 1:25,000
- Sheet 40
  Gross Glockner Group
  Scale 1:25,000

Also useful and available from major map retailers are:

- *Freytag & Berndt Wanderkarte* sheet 152 scale 1:50,000 (Mayrhofen-Zillertaler Alpen-Gerlos-Krimml).
- *Rudolf Rother Wanderkarte* 1:50,000 scale (Glockner, Granatspitz and Venediger groups).

For **guidebooks**, see Appendix C (Further Reading).

ALPINE WALKING SKILLS

So how do the skills you need for walking in the Hohe Tauern differ from those needed for walking elsewhere?

Boots

It really is essential that you have a relatively stiff boot with good ankle support and a stout Vibram-type rubber sole. Many of the walks involve sustained hard walking over rocky slopes and glacial debris plus encounters with patches of old hard snow. It is important to think of your boots as tools that can be used to kick steps and to jam into rocky cracks without

Some basic Alpine walking kit

causing damage to your feet. While bendy boots may be a tad lighter and more comfortable they are no match for a good pair of four-season mountaineering boots when it comes to dealing with difficult ground.

Instep Crampons or Microspikes

While crampons are normally associated with climbing, a pair of these little tools (pictured) comes in very handy when the weather decides to dump some unseasonable snow in August and they may just help provide that little bit of extra security when you get up close to some old hard-packed snow.

Improvised Harness

Many of the routes are equipped with fixed wire ropes to aid some support

Improvised harness

A Tape joint at your back
B Overhand knot tied around the waist
C Overhand knot tied slightly above the knee
D Tightoverhand knot at the end of the sling to hold the karabiner captive

over bits of difficult terrain. While these maybe relatively easy to cross, the consequences of a fall could be serious. Also not everyone is vertigo free and the use of an improvised harness will help provide confidence and security of passage. Constructed from a 2m long x 10mm wide Dyneema sling, three or four overhand knots and a large screw gate karabiner (see picture above), it will allow you to clip into those fixed wires whenever the need arises and arrest a fall when you least expect it!

Trekking Poles

Poles are almost a standard accessory for most folk these days but in the Alps they come into their own, being very handy when crossing glacial steams and for traversing those steep patches of old snow.

Glacier travel

The glaciers of the Hohe Tauern are in the heartland of the Tyrol and the Eastern Alps, with the Gross Venediger's glaciers covering the greatest area, while the Pasterzen Kees glacier adjacent to the Gross Glockner remains the longest single glacier in the Eastern Alps. Quite a few of the mountaineering routes described in this guide involve crossing or negotiating glaciers that can be heavily crevassed, depending on the time of year and varying from season to season.

Crevasses (*spalten*) will be encountered but they should not create a serious problem for the mountain traveller and most will be easily bypassed. As is common to most glaciers, the main crevasse zone will be on the steep sections, at the edges and where the ice breaks away from the underlying rocks to form *bergschrunds, randkluft*. If difficulties do arise it will be in negotiating *bergschrunds* such as those below the

Romariswandkopf on the Fruschnitz Kees glacier.

Orientation on the glacier is described as being in the direction of flow along the right or left-hand bank. This means that in ascent the left bank will be on your right. To avoid confusion, as when route finding in mist, a compass bearing has been added in the route description to aid direction.

Although most of the Hohe Tauern's glaciers are relatively straightforward, they can vary quite considerably from season to season, the Obersulzbach Kees and Umbal glaciers being good examples. This scenario is further exacerbated by large temperature variations generally because of the glaciers' relatively low altitudes. This means that while routes may be straightforward one year, with minimal snowfall in the following year previously hidden crevasses may become exposed and enlarged. The result is that glacier travel becomes more problematic.

The ideal number of people for glacier travel is four. Two is the absolute minimum although two cannot be entirely safe, and solo travel should be avoided. For a party of two some added security could be gained by teaming up with a second party, gaining strength through numbers.

In summer, many of the Hohe Tauern's glaciers are dry glaciers at their lower levels and are quite safe to traverse un-roped, as the crevasses are obvious and easily avoided.

However, when crevasses pose a threat, for example where they

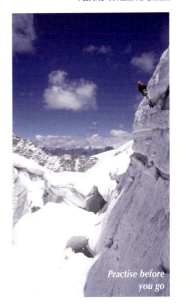

Practise before you go

overlap, are deep or when they occur on steep ground, as will be found on the Reichen Spitze and Gross Venediger, then the party should be roped up. Equally parties should be roped at all times while crossing glaciers that are snow-covered as will be found on the Koednitz Kees glacier on the approach to the Gross Glockner, no matter how well trodden the route. It is worth remembering that crevasses have no respect for people and can open up beneath the best of us.

For a roped party of three, the group leader, the most experienced person, is best placed in the middle, since it is the group leader who will contribute most to a rescue in the

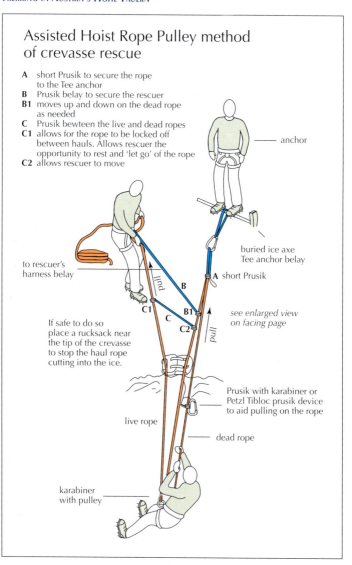

event of a mishap. The second most experienced person should take the lead position at the head of the rope so as to route find, and the last person, preferably the heaviest, should take a place at the back to act as anchorman.

For parties visiting the Alps for the first time, particularly those of equal ability, some experimenting will be necessary to gain more experience. However it is absolutely essential that you practise roping up and crevasse rescue before you go; particularly, practise a crevasse rescue scenario were the fallen climber is out of sight of their companions and when another member of the party has to go to their assistance and enter the crevasse as would be the case if your companion hurts themself.

The following technique is suggested (only suggested because the style varies between German and French parts of the Alps). If you learned glacier and crevasse techniques in the Western Alps you may well have been taught a different but equally valid approach. This method works and will ensure that a group has a safe anchor at all times.

In ascent and descent the lightest person should go first at the front to route find. Should the route finder fall into a crevasse (unlikely) it is improbable that the rest of the group will be dragged in after them, but in a full-on fall you will be dragged off your feet. In case such a mishap occurs then the heaviest person is best placed at the back to act as anchor. For a party of two the most experienced person should be at the back in both ascent and descent.

To rope up a party of three, the middle man (group leader) should tie on 15m from one end of the rope, with the rope leader tied on at the front end. The back man (anchorman) should then tie on about 12m behind the middle man (group leader). The surplus rope at the end should then be coiled by the anchorman and carried over the shoulder and rucksack or, as the author prefers, it can be loosely coiled inside the top of the rucksack from where it can be easily retrieved in the event of being needed for a crevasse rescue. In addition to roping up, two Prusik loops are needed for attaching to the rope by each person, to be stored in their pockets.

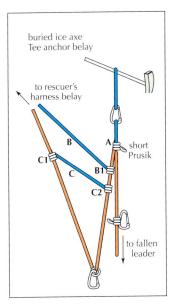

On most glaciers the party will move together, keeping a respectable distance between each person. When there is no crevasse danger a few rope coils may be carried in the hand of each person to make the rope more manageable and to help prevent it snagging and being dragged along the glacier's surface, making the rope wet and heavy.

When crevasse zones are encountered, the rope between individuals should be kept taut to limit the effect of a fall. Where crevasses pose a very real risk, such as when they are large or their extent is unknown, the rope leader's second (middle man) should belay, while the rope leader traverses or jumps the crevasse. At the same time the group's anchorman will be similarly belayed a safe distance away. While these procedures may seem complicated and time-consuming, with a little practice they should become second nature.

The purpose behind these techniques is to prevent climbers falling into crevasses and to ensure glaciers are crossed safely. Most mountaineers will spend many hours crossing glaciers without any serious mishap. Experienced mountaineers will be able to recall falling into crevasses up to the waist, a few to the chest and the odd one falling through the surface to the glacier below. In most instances during a fall climbers can react quickly enough to spread their weight by outstretching their arms or by falling backwards to prevent themselves falling further. Once the fall is arrested, the group's second (the group leader) should belay while the anchorman uses their weight and position to secure the belay which then frees the group leader to make use of the anchorman's coiled spare rope to affect the rescue and haul the leader free.

Should the leader fall free and end up inside the crevasse, it is important the rest of the party work quickly. If falling into a concealed crevasse it is likely the rope leader will be hurt. This is due to the fact that their rucksack will have jarred, pushing the head forward and banging it on the ice during the fall. In such situations there are a number of options to choose from, but all will be useless unless the group has spent a little time practising crevasse rescue techniques. **This is absolutely essential.**

In this situation, provided the rope leader is uninjured it may be possible to:
a) simply haul them out of the crevasse using brute force.
b) help the rope leader to Prusik out of the crevasse under their own steam.
c) by lowering the end of the end of the surplus rope, rescue the rope leader by using a combination of hauling and Prusiking using the assisted Hoist Rope Pulley Method. (See diagram on page 36).

If the rope leader is injured, then the actual group leader will have to go into the crevasse to perform first aid and secure the second haulage rope. Thereafter once the group leader (the middle man if there are three of you) is back on the surface it is just about possible for the group leader and anchorman to haul the rope leader to the surface, using the Prusik loops to lock off the hauling rope. In this scenario a full-blown mountain rescue is perhaps the correct decision.

The UK Section of the Austrian Alpine Club organises basic training for glacier crossing and crevasse rescue through the OeAV Bergsteigerschule. Contact the AAC Office for details.

The National Mountain Centre at Plas y Brenin also runs similar introductory courses. Contact www.pyb.co.uk.

A DVD of 'Alpine Essentials' is also available from the British Mountaineering Council (BMC).

KIT LIST

As a general principle a good rule is: one on, one off. When travelling as a group try to share items that have a commonality of equipment to minimise the weight each person has to carry. For example you will only need one comprehensive first aid kit, one repair kit, one set of maps, one guidebook, one phrase book, one pair of binoculars, and only one set of spare batteries if all the headlamps are the same.

- Rucksack (50 litre)
- Boots (suitable for all seasons)
- Trekking poles (optional)
- Long socks (2 pairs)
- Short socks (2 pairs)
- Trousers or breeches
- Shorts (optional)
- Underwear (3 pairs)
- Shirts (2)
- Pullover
- Fleece jacket
- Waterproofs, jacket and trousers
- Hat, gloves
- Gaiters (optional)
- Torch or headlamp
- Toiletries plus small towel
- Water bottle or Thermos flask

- First aid kit with sun cream and lip salve
- Sunglasses plus spare
- Repair kit: needle and thread, super glue, candle, binding wire
- Pocket knife
- Selection of polythene bags
- Maps and compass
- Whistle
- Notepad and pencil
- *Hohe Tauern* guidebook (this one!)
- Emergency gear, bivvy bag, food rations
- Personal optional items, such as: German phrase book, camera, film, binoculars

TREKKING IN AUSTRIA'S HOHE TAUERN

Statue of Annasaule on Maria Theresien Strasse looking toward the Alte Stadt

KIT LIST

Also recommended for walkers
- 1 set of instep crampons or Microspikes
- 1 2m long x 10mm wide Dyneema tape sling with a large screwgate karabiner

Should you intend to **climb some of the peaks** then you will need to add the following to your kit and know how to use them:
- Ice axe
- Crampons
- 2 large slings with screw gate karabiners
- 3 Prussik loops
- Climber's harness
- Ice screw
- 2 spare karabiners
- A length of climber's rope such as 50m x 9mm for each group of 3 people
- A small selection of slings with nuts/a pulley/universal rock piton

Other items, which are useful (one of each within a group) are:
- Altimeter
- Ice hammer
- Dead boy
- Snow belay
- Figure of eight abseil device
- Prusiking devices such as Petzl Tibloc or Wild Country Ropeman

Hut wear
- Lightweight change of clothes
- Hut shoes or socks
- Trousers
- Shirt
- Sheet sleeping bag
- Inflatable pillow

MOUNTAIN GUIDES

Professional mountain guides (*Bergfuehreren*) can be hired direct through the UK Section of the Austrian Alpine Club, through the British Association of International Mountain Leaders (www.baiml.org), in Mayrhofen through Peter Habeler's Office on Haupt Strasse, in Matrei in Ost Tyrol via the Guide's Office on Rauterplatz (info@bf1.at), and in Kals am Grossglockner via the Guide's Office (info@glocknerfuehrer.at).

I can also recommend my good friends Harry Holl (team-alpin-austria@aon.at), Hannes Bartl (hannes.bartl@aon.at) and Hannes Wettstein, Nr 167, A-6152 Trins, Tyrol, Austria.

THE REICHEN GROUP

The sign on the bridge says 'single file only' but boys will be boys!

INTRODUCTION AND TOPOGRAPHY

This little-known, compact group of mountains is tucked away at the western extremity of the Hohe Tauern National Park merging with the mountains of the Zillertal and the western edge of the Venediger.

Two main valleys split the group: firstly the Zillergrund, which runs above the resort town of Mayrhofen and contains the villages of In der Au and Barenbad; and secondly, on the northern side of the group, running from the small town of Krimml, is the Krimmler Achental valley famed for its three-tiered waterfall, the highest in Europe.

To the north of the group is the main Inn valley, while to the south is the border with Italy and South Tyrol which was annexed to Italy after the First World War.

The group takes its name from its principal mountain, the Reichen Spitze (3303m), which is something of a mini Matterhorn, when viewed from the south. There are another dozen other peaks over 3000m, the most popular being the Wildergerlos Spitze (3280m) and the Richter Spitze (3054m). The group is easily accessible from Mayrhofen and this provides a good starting point for tours leading into the Venediger.

THE REICHEN DWARVES AND THEIR HOARDS

The Reichen Spitze is also said to contain hoards of gold, silver and precious stones treasure which at one time were guarded by the Reichen Dwarves. Rumour has it that the mythical giant the 'Venedigermanndl' from the Venediger raided the mountain and found the treasure. Overcome by greed and weighed down with his booty he fell into a crevasse and was never to be seen again, though the dwarfs continue their search to recover the treasure.

Hut-to-Hut Routes

As with most groups of mountains in Austria the Reichen Group has its own hut-to-hut Rucksack Route which is ideal for groups of mixed ability.

TREKKING IN AUSTRIA'S HOHE TAUERN

INTRODUCTION AND TOPOGRAPHY

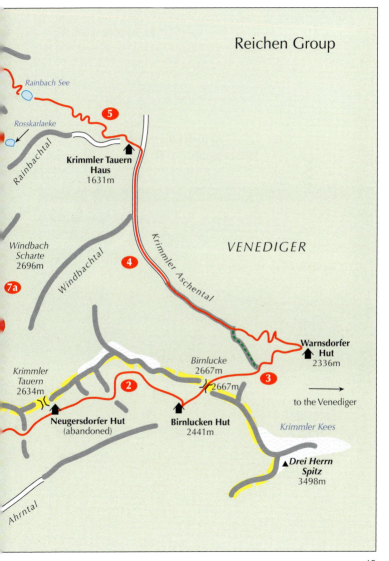

The hut-to-hut route described here is suitable for those with good general ability who are surefooted and vertigo free but who see themselves more as mountain walkers than climbers, free of the burden of rope, axe and crampons and other climbing paraphernalia, as opposed to aspirant alpinists who seek the glaciers and high peaks.

This is a splendid little range and worthy of a visit.

THE REICHEN GROUP HUT-TO-HUT RUCKSACK ROUTE

ROUTE SUMMARY

		Standard time (hrs)	Distance (km)	Ascent (m)
1	Mayrhofen to Plauener Hut	2	3	500
	Excursions from Plauener Hut			
	1.1 Ascent of Reichen Spitze	4–5	>3	930
2	Plauener Hut to Birnlucken Hut	7	12	>1000
3	Birnlucken Hut to Warnsdorfer Hut	4	5	600
4	Warnsdorfer Hut to Krimmler Tauern Haus	2	>6	Nil
5	Krimmler Tauern Haus to Zittauer Hut	4½	7	1100
6	Zittauer Hut to Richter Hut	4	6	500
7A	Richter Hut to Plauener Hut via the Zillerplatten Scharte	7	9	750
7B	Richter Hut to Plauener Hut via the Gams Scharte	4	>3	600

In German the tour is described as the Reichen or Krimmler Rundtour and as a continuous tour will take five to six days to complete, visiting each of the following huts in turn: Plauener, Birnlucken, Warnsdorfer, Krimmler Tauern Haus, Zittauer, Richter, Plauener.

Maps
Austrian Alpine Club Alpenvereinskarte *Zillertaler Alpen Ost* sheet 35/3. 1:25,000 scale. This map covers the whole tour except for one tiny corner near the Warnsdorfer Hut.

Freytag & Bernt sheet 152 *Mayrhofen-Zillertal Alpen-Gerlos-Krimml*. 1:50,000 scale.

Approach
By local bus from the resort town of Mayrhofen at the head of the Zillertal valley: from Mayrhofen *bahnhof* to Zillerplatten at the Zillergrundl *Stausee* (reservoir). Journey time 1hr.
- Outward: 08.30/09.30/10.30/11.30/12.30/14.30/15.30hrs
- Return: 09.25/10.25/11.25/12.25/14.25/15.25hrs

STAGE 1
Mayrhofen to Plauener Hut

Standard time	2hrs
Distance	3km
Ascent	500m

Beginning at the end of the Zillergrundl local bus route, this stage is a simple walk along the shore of the Speicher Zillergrundl reservoir and up the Sonntaglahnerkopf to the Plauener Hut.

From **Mayrhofen** take the local bus service to **Barenbad** in the Zillergrundl valley and then the reservoir dam at Ziller Platten (1hr). ▶

From the **bus terminal** at the reservoir, from where the hut is clearly visible, follow a graded track on **Route 502**, better known as the Zentralalpenweg (Central Alpine Way), through the hydroelectric plant tunnel for 200m,

Look out for avalanche damage caused by a rockfall in 2005 which completely obliterated the tiny alm at Barenbad.

TREKKING IN AUSTRIA'S HOHE TAUERN

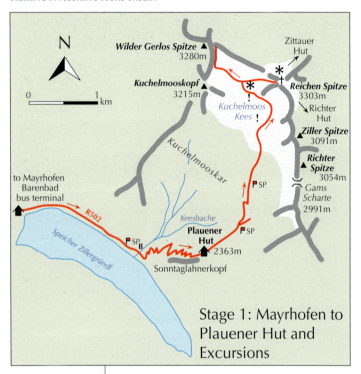

Stage 1: Mayrhofen to Plauener Hut and Excursions

Here is a war memorial to fallen comrades of the DAV and OeAV.

continuing along the well-defined track to where it forks at an obvious junction with a **signpost**. ◄

From here the path steepens, first zigzagging through scrub and alpine rose bushes followed by a crossing of the open rocky ground of the Kuchelmooskar to a single plank **bridge** whose sign requests 'single file only' to get over the **Keesbache** main stream coming down from the Kuchelmoos Kees glacier.

Thereafter the path picks up pace to zigzag to and fro under the cliffs of the **Sonntaglahnerkopf** and on to the hut.

Stage 1 – Excursions from Plauener Hut

EXCURSIONS FROM PLAUENER HUT

Unless you are an aspirant alpinist, excursions from the hut are limited to general rambles, so in that regard the hut offers very little scope to the general mountain wanderer. However once you are armed with a rope, an ice axe and some crampons there is much to entertain and test your skills.

Plauener Hut with the Kuchelmoos Kopf on the left, Wilder Gerlos Spitze in the centre and the Reichen Spitze right of centre

1.1 Ascent of Reichen Spitze (3303m)

Standard time	4 to 5hr
Distance	3+km
Ascent	930m
Grade	PD/II

This is a splendid climb and highly recommended.

From the hut the route is mostly self explanatory and pretty obvious. The climbing is straightforward, varied and interesting without requiring the expenditure of too much nervous energy.

The principal mountain of the group, and home of the Reichen Dwarfs legend, provides a splendid day out starting with a good glacier journey and rock scramble to finish.

From the hut head out northeast picking up the trail signposted for the Gams Scharte. Follow the well-marked trail up the old glacial moraine to a **signpost** after 20mins and another one 1hr, to the Gams Scharte at 2600m, where the trail splits. Hereabouts it will be obvious why the Gams is such a problematic col to cross and why it should be avoided in less than good weather.

The trail of sorts continues north weaving its way through boulders below the **Ziller Spitze** to gain the lower edge and snow fields of the **Kuchelmoos Kees** glacier. ◄ (1½hrs).

> Some of the names that you find in the Eastern Alps are wonderful!

Tackle up and get onto the glacier climbing the steep slopes just off centre of its left bank until roughly level with the ice fall at around 2800m. If previous parties have climbed the mountain then tracks should be obvious through the bank of crevasses to the left, west; if not then continue to climb northeast heading directly for the summit until the slope starts to ease off at 3000m. It would have been hereabouts that the Venedigermanndl would have fallen into a crevasse loaded down with his booty, never to be seen again.

Now head northwest toward the foot of the southwest ridge and the centre of the glacier keeping a safe distance from to steep rock faces in case of rockfall.

Once in the centre of the glacier turn northeast heading for a gap in the ridge at 3142m (1½hrs). The route indicated on the Alpenvereins map up through a snow couloir is steep and not recommended due to the risk of rockfall. Get onto the northwest ridge, keeping right of the crest and scramble up shattered rocks and difficult broken ground, very exposed in places, to the summit with its large wooden cross (1hr).

In descent retrace your steps to get onto the Kuchelmoos Kees glacier and head into the middle of the glacier. Again avoid the temptation to take a short cut down the west couloir which is now much more obvious in descent.

STAGE 1 – EXCURSIONS FROM PLAUENER HUT

Ascent of the Reichen Spitze, Doug Ball high on the Kuchelmoos Kees glacier with the Wilder Gerlos Spitze in the background

Once in the middle of the glacier it is decision time: whether to press on to the **Wildergerlos Spitze** (3278m) or to descend.

If you wish to continue, cross the glacier as before heading for the obvious notch in the ridge at 3125m. You can get rid of ice axe and crampons as you won't need them from here on. Get onto the ridge and follow this to the summit. Good scrambling with short pitches of PD/grade II (2hrs). Return by the same route.

From the centre of the upper glacier basin retrace your steps past the foot of the southwest ridge heading for the west bank of the glacier. Either retrace your steps over the upper snow slope or look to pick a route through the bank of crevasses to the left of the main ice-fall and then down the last snow slopes to the boulder field below and back to the hut.

REICHEN SPITZE SUMMIT

The scenery throughout – in ascent and descent – is excellent, particularly from the summit where there are good views down adjacent valleys to the Richter Hut, the Zittauer Hut and back down to the Plauener Hut, then across the void to the Warnsdorfer Hut and Venediger Group. While on the summit look for the charred remains of the old wooden cross which was burnt to a crisp by a lightning strike – such is the raw power of nature.

Apart from weather considerations, the main risk is of over-extending oneself by trying to climb both mountains in the day when not fit enough.

In terms of climbing, the glacier crossing is straightforward without serious crevasse danger. However once on the ridges, climbing is very exposed with jaw-dropping exposure in a couple of places while negotiating steep difficult broken ground, which is more problematic in descent.

STAGE 2
Plauener Hut to Birnlucken Hut

Standard time	7hrs
Distance	12km
Ascent	A lot of up and down

This mountain journey is characterised simply as being a long way. The standard time is 7hrs which is fine if you are fit, however if you are carrying a big bag allow all day, be on your way early and telephone the Birnlucken hut to book a bed.

This is a splendid long-distance promenade through fabulous scenery with nice little challenges thrown in. The scenic interest early in the day is dominated by the Rauchkofel (3252m) which may take its name for its rough-jagged ridges, or maybe because of the way the cloud hangs from its north face like woodsmoke, hence the name, 'Smoking Mountain'; my preference is for the latter.

Thereafter the route becomes hemmed in as the head of the Zillergrundl narrows until the crossing of the Geistjochl (2708m) into Italy, when the Ahrntal valley opens up. Hereafter the route picks up a trail traversing the mountainside, crossing four spurs, each quite steep and each protected by fixed wire ropes to aid stability.

After crossing the second ridge the rest of the journey is scenically dominated by the vastness of the Drei Herrn Spitz or Picco del tre Signori (3498m) with its jagged ridges and hanging glaciers.

At the Geistjochl looking back into Austria and Zillergrundl

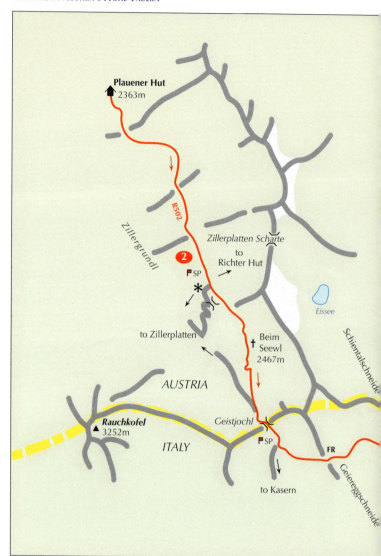

STAGE 2 – PLAUENER HUT TO BIRNLUCKEN HUT

Stage 2: Plauener Hut to the Birnlucken Hut

En route to the Birnlucken Hut with the Rauchkofel on the left skyline

From the Plauener Hut, the path sets off following a rocky trail in a southerly direction on Route 502, better known as the Zentralalpenweg (Central Alpine Way), towards the head of the Zillergrundl valley.

After 1½hrs a junction is reached with a **signpost** indicating the route over the Zillerplatten Scharte to the Richter Hut. Good views hereabouts across the void to the Rauchkofel (3252m), alternatively known as the 'Smoking Mountain', and back down the valley to the *Stausee* (reservoir). This spot will be crossed again in about a week or so when undertaking the return journey from the Richter Hut.

The path continues to climb over rocks then unfortunately turns to descend and loses a hundred metres or so in height, dropping down into the glacial basin at **Beim Seewl**. ◂

This is an excellent spot for a second breakfast.

Thereafter the path heads up through glacial debris and moraines climbing and zigzagging through rocks to emerge on the col at **Geistjochl** (2708m) and the border between Austria and Italy.

STAGE 2 – PLAUENER HUT TO BIRNLUCKEN HUT

> Not so long ago this area would have been patrolled by border police and had you been in the area at that time you would have been escorted off the mountain. The only permitted border crossing into Italy during those difficult times was the Brenner Pass.
>
> On a good day you will be rewarded with good views of the Ahrntal valley and the spectacular Drei Herrn Spitz (3498m), one of the major peaks in the region.

From the col descend difficult ground over rocks and shale to a junction of paths with a **signpost** (15mins). From here on you will be on Route 13 all the way to the Birnlucken Hut.

From the signpost continue to traverse across the mountainside in an easterly direction crossing the the **Geiereggschneide**, the first of four ridges, at 2466m on the Lausitzer Weg approximately ½hr from the Geistjochl.

Descend the initial steep rocks, with **fixed wires** in place, and contour around to the next ridge **Schientalschneide** (½hr).

As you round the corner of the ridge both the Birnlucken Hut and the abandoned Neugersdorfer Hut come into view. Descend steep ground, more **fixed wires** in place, and continue the journey to a junction of several paths below the **Neugersdorfer Hut** and the trail leading back over the Krimmler Tauern into Austria (1hr). ▶

From the Neugersdorfer, with the Birnlucken Hut clearly in view, the route continues as before and sets out to cross the third ridge, the **Taurschneide**, descending steep ground with **fixed wires**, and onto the fourth and last ridge the **Pfaffenschneide**, crossing it at the Teufelssteige (2526m) via an interesting timber staircase (1hr).

The route descends, making use of the now familiar fixed wires, then crosses rocky slabs, boulders and easier ground to the hut (½hr).

> This is a good place to stop for lunch and ponder the fate of the Neugersdorfer Hut, as well as the logistics of bringing cattle up from the Ahrntal valley over the Krimmler Tauern pass.

The main characteristic of the journey is that it is simply a long way with lots of up and down. Because of this it is not a route to undertake on a falling barometer or in poor weather when route finding would be made more difficult, along with the added difficulty of negotiating the steep ground and fixed wires when crossing each of the ridges.

Because of the length of the route general fitness to undertake the journey carrying a full rucksack will play an important part in the enjoyment of the day. While 7hrs is generally the standard time, participants should allow all day and be on their way early. Fortunately the route has a number of escape routes on the Italian side of the journey should the need arise. These are: first from the Geistjochl (2708m) on the Austrian Italian border; and second from the abandoned Neugersdorfer Hut, each descending to Kasern or St Peter's in the Ahrntal valley. I would add that the journey times from the Neugersdorfer down into the valley or onto the Birnlucken hut are the same: only the ground differs, so unless you are absolutely desperate and being battered by the weather it is probably just as easy to continue to the hut.

NEUGERSDORFER HUT

Also known as the Krimmler Tauern Hut and Rifugio Vetta d'Italia.

This splendid hut situated overlooking the Ahrntal valley was built by the Warnsdorf *Sektion* in 1907, was lost to Italy in 1919 then handed to the Italian Alpine Club in 1919. It was retained by the Italian Army up to 1970, when it was abandoned in a ruinous state.

The hut, apart from its usefulness for mountaineering, is strategically located on ancient trade routes between the Zillertal and Ahrntal communities particularly used for driving cattle over the Krimmler Tauern pass (2634m), all of which came to an abrupt end after the First World War.

Hopefully the CAI or some local entrepreneur will find the energy to see the hut reopen to mountain travellers in the not too distant future.

STAGE 3
Birnlucken Hut to Warnsdorfer Hut

Standard time	4hrs
Distance	5km
Ascent	600m

A good day's outing whose scenic interest is wholly dominated by the Drei Herrn Spitze or Picco del tre Signori (3498m) and the expanse of the Krimmler Kees glacier. This is an excellent promenade aided by superb scenery and no obstacles to warrant a cautionary note. Enjoy!

From the Birnlucken Hut continue to follow Route 13 up the rocky northeast ridge for a short hour to the **Birnlucke pass** (2667m) marking the border between Austria and Italy.

At the Birnlucken pass looking into Italy and the Ahrntal valley

TREKKING IN AUSTRIA'S HOHE TAUERN

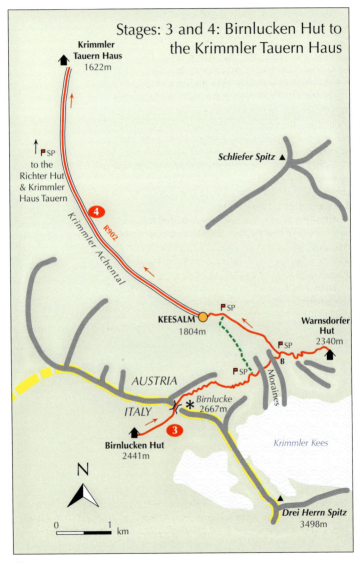

From here there is a good view toward the Warnsdorfer Hut, the extensive **Krimmler Kees** glacier and the mile-long ridge leading from the Simony Spitze all the way to the **Drei Herrn Spitz**. Also look out for extensive glacial moraines in the valley which in the early morning light give the illusion of being a lake. Sharp eyes on a good day will also locate the Warndorfer Hut situated on a rocky rib and the very distinctive snow-covered ridge of the Gross Venediger (3660m), the highest peak in the region and fourth highest in Austria.

From the col descend steeply over easy ground for 1hr through high alpine pasture with lots of flowers to the junction of paths, our route taking a short cut across old **glacial moraines** to the **signpost**.

Cross the moraines up and down to and fro crossing a number of **bridges** along the way to the junction of path with **Route 902**. Good scenery down the Krimmler Achental valley and a good place to take a relaxing break before heading off to the hut (1hr).

From roughly the 2000m contour the trail picks up with a number of steepish zigzags in places but always with the hut in view (1hr+).

STAGE 4

Warnsdorfer Hut to Krimmler Tauern Haus

Standard time	2hrs
Distance	6+km
Ascent	Nil (all downhill)

At this stage of the Rucksack Route you must decide whether to have a leisurely stroll down to the Krimmler Tauern Haus or to have a fairly strenuous day and undertake Stage 4 and 5 as a single journey. Only you can decide.

If you have time on your hands my advice would be to make the journey as two separate stages as it is better not to feel under pressure and to spend that little bit of extra time looking at the very scenery we have come to see!

> From the Warnsdorfer Hut descend Route 519 following a well-defined path to the road head, then along a graded single track road through pleasant alpine scenery of the Krimmler Achental valley passing signs for the Richter Hut along the way.

STAGE 5
Krimmler Tauern Haus to Zittauer Hut

Standard time	4½hrs
Distance	7km
Ascent	1100m

Despite having your back to the mighty Drei Herrn Spitz and its dramatic glaciers, the walk down through the Krimml Achental valley is very pretty indeed and is everything that an alpine valley should be, with chalet-style farm buildings, grazing cows, the beauty of the forest, a swiftly flowing river and if you are lucky trout fishermen who may provide your evening meal!

Once past the Krimmler Tauern Haus you are back into the familiar territory of the high alp and the demands this makes on us.

The route to the Rainbach Scharte is particularly fine and if you are blessed with good weather the scenery from Rainbach See is hard to beat with all the adjacent peaks mirrored on its surface. Thereafter the demands of the Rainbach Scharte will get the heart rate going as the difficulties of fixed ropes and very steep ground are overcome. Reaching the col with its splendid views down to the Zittauer Hut and across the glaciated slopes to the Reichen Spitze provides this promenade with its 'wow' factor and the essential challenge of the day.

STAGE 5 – KRIMMLER TAUERN HAUS TO ZITTAUER HUT

From the Krimmler Tauern Haus the route picks up a trail adjacent to the hut and follows a steep forest trail for 1hr, to the **signpost**, then through receding forest and scrub for a further hour to the **Rainbach See** (2410m). ▶

The trail now heads northwest into an obvious cirque of mountains over rocks and boulders then bits of snow leading to the **Rainbach Scharte** (2720m). Below the col the route steepens considerably climbing through via ferrata/klettersteig-style **fixed ropes** for about 100m. If you have your sling and karabiner to construct an improvised harness, you are advised to wear it, if not you need to choose your route carefully (1½hrs).

From the col descend a rock staircase-type trail for 1hr to the hut, passing the junction of paths from the Richter Hut midway.

The pleasant scenery hereabouts makes this a good place to rest and photograph.

VIEW FROM THE RAINBACH SCHARTE

The Zittauer Hut and Gerlos See are clearly visible to the west together with an excellent view of the steep glacier slopes of the Reichen Spitze. And for those with excellent, eagle-eye vision the Warnsdorfer Hut can be seen to the southeast.

The Krimmler Tauern Haus to the Zittauer Hut with the Reichenspitze on the left

TREKKING IN AUSTRIA'S HOHE TAUERN

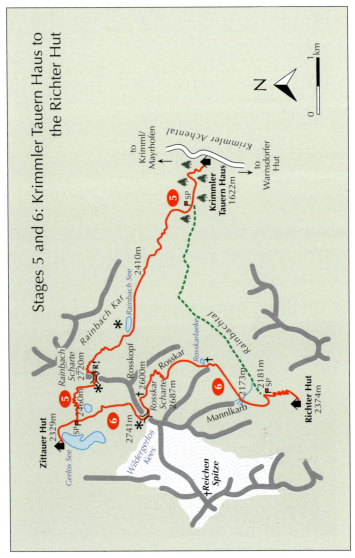

This is not a route to undertake in poor weather for two reasons. First, the vegetated slopes of the upper forest frequently become overgrown, making route-finding more problematic in mist. Second, the climb up to the Rainbach Scharte, while protected by fixed ropes is very steep and needs to be approached with care: it is not a place to be caught out in poor weather or a thunderstorm. If you are in a group it is important to stay together to avoid dislodging rocks on each other and to provide assistance to each other when needs be.

STAGE 6
Zittauer Hut to Richter Hut

Standard time	4hrs
Distance	6km
Ascent	500m

A very pleasant day's outing, with very little to stretch one's mountaineering skills. The highlight of the day is reaching the Rosskar Scharte which has an unrivalled view across the glacial slopes of the Reichen Spitze. Enjoy!

From the Zittauer Hut retrace yesterday's path, following the well-marked trail south over rocks and boulders to the **signpost** at a junction of paths at 2460m leading over the Rainbach Scharte (2720m) (15mins).

Continue south over similar ground with the path rising steadily to reach the high point on the ridge at 2741m and the signpost for the adjacent peak, the **Rosskopf** (2873m). ▶

From here there are excellent views across the Wildergerlos Kees glacier slopes to the Reichen Spitze.

The path descends a short distance over steep ground to a tiny notch in the ridge which marks the **Rosskar Scharte** (2687m) (1hr).

Passing the col, the path descends for a few hundred metres hugging the base of a series of cliffs. Hereafter the path descends over and through the rocks and car-sized boulders of the Rosskar on the eastern flank of the *Reichen Spitze* to a tiny lake, the **Rosskarlaeke** (2291m) (1hr). ◄

> On a good day the hut is clearly visible from here.

From the lake continue as before in a southwesterly direction over rocks and boulders crossing a major stream, the **Mannlkarb**, at 2173m. Across the void the service road to the hut becomes more obvious. After a short distance the path turns across the hillside to meet the road via a footbridge at a **signpost** (1hr).

The trail now follows an obvious path zigzagging its way to the Richter Hut (½hr).

This promenade is relatively straightforward with few obstacles. However in poor visibility the area around the Rosskar boulder field and streams at the Mannlkarb demand that little extra navigational care to avoid losing the track, as the familiar route markings with daubs of red paint are in places infrequent and none too obvious.

The Richter Hut with the service road at the head of the Rainbachtal

STAGE 7A

*Richter Hut to Plauener Hut
via the Zillerplatten Scharte*

Standard time	7hrs
Distance	9km
Ascent	750m

This mountain journey is another characterised as a long way with a fair amount of up and down. However, once across the Windbach Scharte the route opens up to expanse of the Windbachtal valley to provide very enjoyable alpine walking.

Unfortunately once across the Windbach Scharte you are in sort of a mountain no man's land caught at the extreme edges of the Venediger and the Zillertal with all the big peaks hidden from view. Having said that, this remains a very good walk with plenty of scenic interest. The area around the Eissee is particularly fine and makes an ideal stop off point for lunch and photographs before making the last few metres of ascent up to the Zillerplatten Scharte, which has its 'wow' factor and once again provides that instant visual impact of the big mountains we have come to see.

Crossing the Zillerplatten Scharte also marks the last of all the little challenges that have had to be overcome to complete this fine journey through the Reichen group of mountains.

From the hut the route heads out south through glacial debris and the boulder slopes of the Rainbachkeeskar to a small lake (at 2406m) which provides the hut's water supply.

The trail now turns east, steepening and climbing over blocks and slabs in a series of long looping zig-zags to make a rising traverse to the first objective of the day, the Windbach Scharte West or Schontaljochl (2693m), the top section of which is aided by fixed wires (1hr).

STAGE 7A – RICHTER HUT TO PLAUENER HUT

After a final look over our the shoulder for a last view of the Richter Hut and Reichen Group of mountains the scenery for the next hour or so will be dominated by views up the Windbachtal valley and high col of the Krimmler Tauern, from where not so long ago cattle would have been driven and traded between the communities of the Ahrntal, Zillertal and Venediger valleys.

From the col, round the top of the buttress and traverse the exposed track for a short distance, then descend steeply for 100m and 10 mins, using the fixed wires in place to aid stability, to pick up the trail again continuing south to the foot of an obvious ridge, the **Keesfeldschneide** (2600m) (1hr).

The route now follows the 2500m contour south for 1hr or so across open boulder slopes of the Keesfeld rounding a prominent ridge coming down from the **Aschbichlschneide** followed by a short distance to a **signpost** at a junction of paths coming up from the Windbachtal valley and over from the Krimmler Tauern from Italy and the Ahrntal (1hr).

The route continues west, first through a series of zigzags to the very picturesque glacial lake of **Eissee**, then

At the Eissee with Drei Herrn Spitz in the background

turns north, then west, rising gradually over large impressive slabby rocks to get round the glacial amphitheatre of the **Kesselkees**, heading for an obvious col and notch in the ridge marked by a large circular splash of red and white paint.

Just below the col the path steepens to climb the last few metres to the **Zillerplatten Scharte** (2874m) and the main objective of the day (1½hr).

> The **Zillerplatten Scharte** is a tiny col, just about big enough to accommodate two people, with extensive views in all directions particularly down to the Eissee and Ahrntal valley and across the void to the Drei Herrn Spitze, while on the Austrian side the Stausee and Rauchkofel come once again into view.

From the col the route continues as Route 502 on the Central Alpine Way and descends an obvious trail for 400m over rocks and boulders, some of which are nicely paved over, through the open slopes of the Keeskar to a **signpost** at 2475m, where the main track joins paths coming up from the valley and heading to the Ahrntal in Italy (1hr). ◄

Those with reasonable memories will remember passing this spot a week or so ago en route for the Geistjochl and Birnlucken Hut

The route now continues more or less north along a good but rocky path to the Plauener Hut to close the loop and complete the Reichen Rundtour or Rucksack Route (1¼hrs).

> Because of the length of the journey it is obviously not a walk to do in poor weather conditions. The main difficulties come early in the day in crossing the Windbach Scharte where the descent down the rock buttress, while short, is very steep and exposed. Thereafter the terrain is quite straightforward with few difficulties.

STAGE 7B
Richter Hut to Plauener Hut via the Gams Scharte

Standard time	4hrs
Distance	3+km
Ascent	600m
See map on page 68.	

A straightforward journey with a sting. This is a superb journey as it is both challenging and rewarding in equal measure. Since the Gams is high the views are excellent particularly on the Plauener side across the expanse of the Kuchelmoos Kees glacier to the Wildergerlos Spitze. Equally because the Gams is challenging there are plenty of good mountain situations.

From the Richter Hut the Gams Scharte (2991m) is clearly visible as a tiny notch in the ridge between the Richter

Route for the Gams Sharte

Spitze and the Nordl Schwarzkopf. From the hut follow Route 512 signposted in a westerly direction on an obvious trail.

The path rises a tad over 600m in 1.5km, starting off gradually, then, on the 2600m contour, steepening considerably, zigzagging in close succession to ascend the rocky rib of the **Richter Spitze**, the top section of which, leading to the Gams Scharte, is equipped with **fixed ropes** (2½hrs).

THE GAMS SCHARTE

There are good views of the Rainbach Group during the ascent, then further afield to the Drei Herrn Spitze and Gross Venediger, then, once on the col, there are excellent views of the Wildergerlos Spitze (3280m) and attendant Kuchelmoos Kees glacier. At the col both the Richter and Plauener Huts are visible and on a good day those with sharp eyes will be able to see the Warnsdorfer Hut to the southeast.

At the col is a tiny wooden shelter whose sole purpose is to provide emergency shelter as the Plauener side of the col is no place to be caught in bad weather. Sadly the little hut is in need of some tender loving care if it is to perform its function as a shelter.

If you ascended the col using trekking poles then these need to be stowed away as they will be of little use and will hinder your descent from the col.

From the col descend very steep difficult rocky ground making use of **fixed wires** and metal staples to descend the rocky ridge (of sorts) for 150m to reach permanent snow cover and the lower remnants of the Kuchelmooskees glacier.

Progress over this difficult ground is painfully slow to maintain control and to remain safe and will at best take close to 1hr unless you are extremely agile over steep difficult ground.

STAGE 7B – RICHTER HUT TO PLAUENER HUT

From the foot of the ridge the snowfield is guarded by a *bergschrund* of sorts which is crossed making use of a fixed rope. This manoeuvre requires care as the snow slope, while relatively safe, is steep and a fall would be difficult to stop: if you have an ice axe and crampons it would be a wise decision to use them.

Once on the snowfield proceed southwest for 500m or so to cross the snow; thereafter follow a well-marked rocky rib, with the hut in view, to the Plauener Hut (1½hrs).

> Because of the nature of the Gams Scharte it is imperative that the route is undertaken in either direction in good weather only. Crossing the Gams should also be avoided if there has been a fresh snowfall. The Plauener Hut side of the Gams involves very steep broken ground centred around a vague ridge and a gulley. While relatively short (about 150m) the whole of this section is provided with fixed ropes and metal staples fixed to the rocks to form ladders; it is not the place for those who are not vertigo-free and surefooted.
>
> Hut information signs are also woefully inadequate for the journey. At the Plauener Hut the signpost says: '2½hrs to the Gams, 3hrs to the Richter Hut'. If this is so then you have half an hour to descend the 1½km and 600m to the hut – tough going unless you are an athlete!

THE VENEDIGER GROUP

INTRODUCTION AND TOPOGRAPHY

Deep in the heart of the Hohe Tauern National Park, the Venediger Group has the largest covering of glaciers in the Eastern Alps and takes its name from the group's principal mountain, the fourth highest peak in Austria, the Gross Venediger (3660m), which in turn takes its name from the splendid city of Venice.

The valleys which split the group are the Virgental in the south, with host villages of Pragraten, Matrei and Virgen. The Amertal and Tauerntal valleys to the east effectively split the Venediger from the Granat and Gross Glockner Groups. On the northern side run the Inn and Pinzgau valleys, with the premier ski resort of Kitzbuhel; and, lastly, to the west, the Krimmler Achental valley divides the Venediger from the Reichen Group and the Zillertal.

The heavily-glaciated Gross Venediger (3660m) dominates the range but there are another dozen other peaks over 3000m such as the Gross Geiger (3360m) and the challenging Drei Herrn Spitz (3499m).

This is a first class group of mountains.

Hut-to-Hut Routes

There are not many opportunities for glacier free hut-to-hut touring in the Venediger due to the expanse of glaciers associated with the main peaks and central massif; so whatever direction you are travelling in, a glacier will have to be crossed at some stage of the journey.

Several opportunities exist for linear travel through the group either north or south of the Gross Venediger. There are also the Venediger Hoehen Weg and the Sankt Poltener Weg, but these are more or less limited to the southern aspects of the group.

My recommendation for the best combination is to opt for a circular tour taking in the best of the Gross Venediger, with relatively easy glacier crossings and opportunities to climb some of the peaks.

TREKKING IN AUSTRIA'S HOHE TAUERN

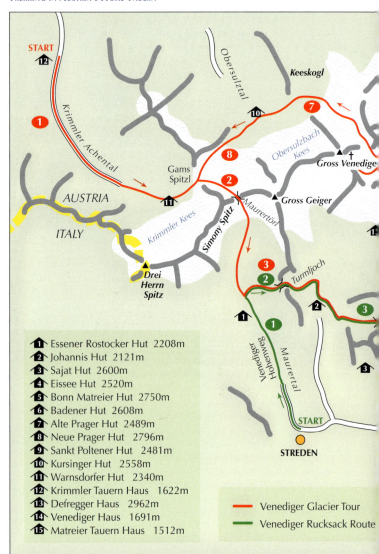

INTRODUCTION AND TOPOGRAPHY

As in my other Alpine trekking guidebooks the route names indicate clearly what type of route is described and what mountaineering skills will be required. The Rucksack Route requires no greater skills than those needed to wander safely over the mountain areas of Britain, whereas a Glacier Tour indicates that participants need to have the ability to cross glaciers safely using ropes, ice axes and crampons.

Rucksack Route

This route of seven continuous days combines the best of the Venediger, and generally follows the Venediger Hoehen Weg and Sankt Poltener Weg. It traverses the Venediger from south to north, starting in the Virgental valley at the Essener Rostocker Hut and prodeeds to each of the following huts: Johannis, Bonn Matreier via the Eissee Hut then Badener, Neue Prager and Sankt Poltener, to end at the Matreier Tauern Haus.

For those with sufficient time on their hands the journey can then continue through the Granat and Gross Glockner Groups: see the chapters on the Glockner Group Rucksack Route and Appendix D, Across the Hohe Tauern National Park.

Glacier Tour

This route of eight continuous days is better suited to mountaineers, particularly those visiting the Alps for the first time, as it takes in the very best of the Venediger, traversing the range on the inner circle in an anti-clockwise direction starting at the Warnsdorfer Hut then to each of the following huts: Essener Rostocker, Johannis, Badener, Neue Prager, Kursinger, then back to the Warnsdorfer to complete the circle. There are opportunities to climb several of the local peaks along the way.

THE VENEDIGER GROUP HUT-TO-HUT RUCKSACK ROUTE

ROUTE SUMMARY

		Standard time (hrs)	Distance (km)	Ascent (m)
1	Matrei in Ost Tyrol to Essener Rostocker Hut	3	5	800
2	Essener Rostocker Hut to Johannis Hut	4	4	670
3	Johannis Hut to Bonn Matreier Hut	7	8	1100
4	Bonn Matreier Hut to Badener Hut	5–6	7	600
5	Badener Hut to Neue Prager Hut	4–6	7	>700
	Excursions from Neue Prager Hut 5.1 Ascent of the Gross Venediger	4	4	870
5A	Badener Hut to Venediger Haus Alternative bad weather route	4	>8	Nil
6	Neue Prager Hut to Sankt Poltener Hut	7	>14	>600
7	Sankt Poltener Hut to Matreier Tauern Haus	3	6	Nil

This tour traverses the Venediger from south to north, starting in the Virgental valley, at Streden, then visiting each of the following huts: Essener Rostocker, Johannis, Bonn Matreier via the Eissee Hut, then Badener, Neue Prager and Sankt Poltener and ending at the Matreier Tauern Haus. The journey can be continued into the Granat Group and the mountains of the Gross Glockner.

Maps

Austrian Alpine Club Alpenvereinskarte *Venedigergruppe* Sheet 36. 1:25,000 scale.

Rudolf Rother Wanderkarte 1:50,000 scale (Glockner, Granatspitz and Venediger groups).

En-route to the Turmljoch

Getting there and back

From Innsbruck by train to Kitzbuhel, then by regional bus to Matrei in Ost Tyrol and local bus to Hinterbichl, followed by a taxi as far as the material/goods hoist for the Essener Rostocker Hut. The normal train from Innsbruck at 09:25hrs throughout the week links up with the bus from Kitzbuhel at 10:35hrs, arriving in Matrei at 12:18hrs.

Local buses along the Virgental valley to Hinterbichl are roughly every hour (09.41/11.41/12.41/13/41/14.41/15.41/16.51hrs) and take about 1hr. A taxi from Hinterbichl to Streden and up to the materials hoist where the road ends. Taxis are available from Venediger Taxis 04877 5369/5231

If you are ending the tour as described you need to be at the bus stop at Matreier Tauern Haus no later than 10.00hrs, since the bus leaves at 10:10hrs. The local bus service from Matrei (13.45hrs) arrives at Kitzbuhel at 15:03hrs. The train from Kitzbuhel (15:19hrs) arrives at Innsbruck at (16:26hrs).

STAGE 1
Matrei in Ost Tyrol to Essener Rostocker Hut

Standard time	3hrs from Streden or 1½hrs from the *seilbahn* (materials hoist)
Distance	5km
Ascent	800m

STAGE 1 – MATREI IN OST TYROL TO ESSENER ROSTOCKER HUT

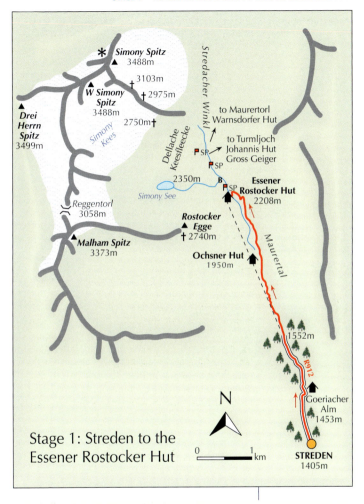

See hut directory for information on the Essener Rostocker Hut and 'Getting there and back' for general transport details.

If you want to **avoid the taxi journey** up the valley, from the hamlet of Streden follow Route 912 north along a well-frequented trail up through the forest of the Maurertal valley. It is pleasant walking first along a single track graded road past the chalet and farm buildings at Maurer Alm then up to the *seilbahn* where the road ends at 1552m above Goeriacher Alm.

From the seilbahn continue as before through the forest, the road eventually giving way to a well-worn track and then leaving the forest behind at Ochsnerhuette (1950m) for the last 300m of uphill to the hut.

See the Venediger Glacier Tour for excursions from the Essener Rostocker Hut (page 110).

STAGE 2

Essener Rostocker Hut to Johannis Hut via the Turmljoch (2790m)

Standard time	4hrs
Distance	4km
Ascent	670m

A very pleasant straightforward day's outing, with little to hinder one's progress, if somewhat short in duration.

From the hut follow Route 913 up the Stredbach valley to a **signpost**. After a short distance the path crosses the first of two footbridges over the glacial streams of the Maurerbach. Continue as before and after 20 minutes you will come to a **signpost** and a second **footbridge** indicating the way over the **Turmljoch**.

The route turns east climbing steadily in a series of zigzags on a good path following the Schmeriner Weg to the pass (2hrs).

Stage 2 – Essener Rostocker Hut to Johannis Hut

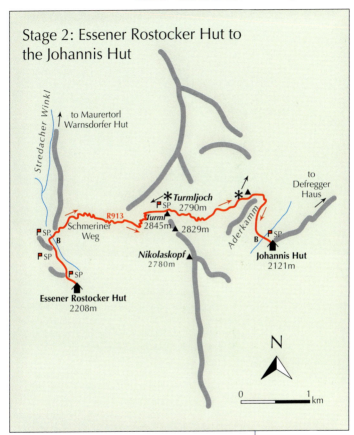

At the pass, take time out to enjoy the view back across the void to the Drei Herrn Spitz and the Simony group of mountains which will now consigned to the past once on the far side of the Turmljoch.

The pass is also home to large groups of **Edelweiss** and vivid blue **Spring Gentian**. If you have not seen the elusive Edelweiss before now is your opportunity.

The Turmljoch rock tower

You will also have the opportunity to climb the actual **Turmljoch tower** (2845m), after which the pass is named, following the protected *klettersteig* (climbing path) if you have with you the necessary climbing gear (harness and slings), otherwise just sit back and enjoy the pass before moving on. Excellent scenery.

From the pass descend through the **Aderkamm**, following a well-marked trail indicated by a number of well-constructed stone cairns.

After ½hr or so the service road to the hut becomes obvious and not long after that the hut comes into view along with the Rainerhorn satellite peak of the Gross Venediger to the north. Once on the valley floor stop to admire the forces of nature, specifically the natural footbridge that has been blasted through the rock by the powers of raging glacial water, followed by a short stroll to the hut (1½hrs).

STAGE 3

*Johannis Hut to Bonn Matreier Hut
via the Zopat Scharte and Eissee Hut*

Standard time	7hrs
Distance	8km
Ascent	1100m

This is a good long distance trail with a fair amount of up and down made less demanding with a good interlude for lunch at the pleasant Eissee Hut, and while quite long it is not over-demanding. The highlight of the day is the absolutely superb walking contouring around the head of the Virgental valley which is stunning, with southern slopes covered in high alpine flowers and continuous views across the valley to the Lasorling group of mountains.

From the Johannis Hut, the trail heads east continuing to follow Route 923 and the Venediger Hoehen Weg, heading up and across the grassy slopes of the Zettalurilzach to the junction of paths leading to the **signpost** at the Sajat Hut (1hr).

Continue east as before, following the well marked trail and, ignoring signs for the Sajat Hut which follow in quick succession, enter the boulder-strewn slopes and

Simony Group from the Zopat Scharte

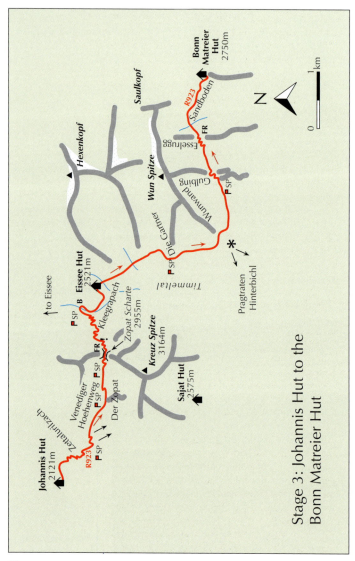

STAGE 3 – JOHANNIS HUT TO BONN MATREIER HUT

couloir of the Zopat at 2700m, with the Zopat Scharte (2955m) clearly visible ahead (½hr).

From here onwards retrospective views of the Drei Herrn Spitz and Simony mountains are lost.

Continue as before following the now rocky trail that gradually steepens through a series of zigzags to the col with views back across the void to the Gross Geiger and the previously crossed Turmljoch. Ahead is the glacial basin that forms Eissee (1hr). From the col descend northeast.

The first 100m is exceedingly steep down slopes of loose shale with rock flakes on edge, with **fixed wires** in place but still demanding care until the ground eases at 2800m.

From here onwards the Eissee is clearly visible, as is the continuing path on the far side of the valley which will eventually take us to the Bonn Matreier Hut. Continue to descend the slopes of the **Kleegrapach** via a series of zigzags to the convergence of streams pouring down from Eissee and on to the Eissee Hut (2521m) (1hr, 3½hrs hut-to-hut). ▶

From Eissee Hut, descend down the valley for a couple of hundred metres following the obvious trail until a signpost is reached which indicates the way to the Bonn Matreier Hut.

The route now heads southeast roughly following the 2500m contour, across the hillside high above the Timmeltal valley providing almost effortless delightful walking for a short hour when a superbly constructed rock staircase near a **signpost** is reached at **Die Gartner** (¾hr).

The trail now rounds the corner of the Wunwand's southern buttress, continuing as before to provide very pleasant walking, contouring the slopes high above the Virgental valley, and the little town of Pragraten in particular, for the next 1¼hrs until your leisurely progress is stopped in its tracks by the ridge of the **Gulbing**, where there is a **signpost**.

Climb the steep little slope in a series of very tight zigzags to the col from where our next task comes into

This little hut is a convenient place to enjoy an early lunch.

view. Descend from the col and cross the rocky slopes of the **Grubach,** climbing steadily to the obvious col on the ridge and the donkey's back of the **Esselrugg** (2660m) from where the **Bonn Matreier Hut** comes into view situated on its rock promontory just 1km away (½hr).

From the col descend the very steep slope making use of the **fixed ropes** until the ground eases to cross the rocky slopes and streams of the **Sandboden** and the last final pull up to the hut (1hr, 3½hrs hut-to-hut).

While a relatively straightforward journey one place that requires mention is the descent from the Zopat Scharte which, although short and protected by fixed ropes, descends very steep difficult broken ground. If you are in a group, participants should stay close together, and those who are not entirely vertigo-free should enlist the help of a friend.

The only other requirement is that because the route is quite long, it is not one to undertake in poor weather. Having said that, the route can be split into two by making an overnight stay at the very pleasant Eissee Hut, a worthwhile consideration if you have children with you.

STAGE 4

Bonn Matreier Hut to Badener Hut via the Galten Scharte (2882m)

Standard time	5–6hrs
Distance	7km
Ascent	600m

STAGE 4 – BONN MATREIER HUT TO BADENER HUT

This is the hardest and most challenging day of the Venediger Rucksack Route. Signs outside the hut state that the crossing of the Galten Scharte is for the experienced only and that you should enquire from the hut warden about local conditions before committing to the route.

But despite the grotty nature of the Galten Scharte this is a very good day's outing full of scenic variety and challenge. The ascent to the Galten Scharte via the Kalber Scharte is particulary good and very enjoyable.

The Galten Scharte itself is in a fine situation with excellent scenery down the Frosnitztal valley and across the void to the east and mountains of the Granat Group and Grosser Muntanitz. Unfortunately views toward the Gross Venediger and other high peaks remain hidden from view.

It is the walk across the grassy slopes of the Galderet which is particularly fine with alpine walking not coming much better than this and in total contrast to the rigours of the Galten Scharte.

From the hut head off north on Route 922, signposted, on a good track in the direction of the Saulkopf to the junction of various paths where there is a **signpost** (5mins).

The route now loops round to the right, traversing boulder slopes, to a sign 'Badener Hut' painted on the

Negotiating steep ground at the Galten Scharte

TREKKING IN AUSTRIA'S HOHE TAUERN

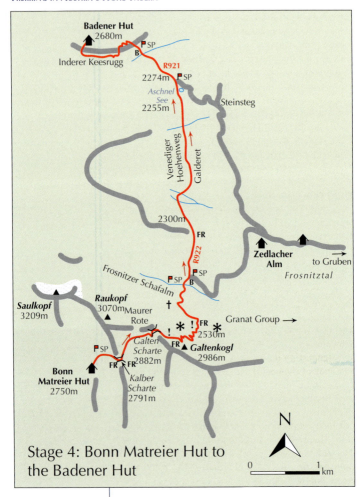

Stage 4: Bonn Matreier Hut to the Badener Hut

boulders in big letters and showing the way to the Kalber Scharte (2791m). Climb steepening slopes over block boulders heading into a narrow cleft aided by **fixed wires** and man-made steps to the head of the tiny col (20 mins).

Stage 4 – Bonn Matreier Hut to Badener Hut

An excellent situation in a true mountain setting. The Galten Scharte is visible across the cirque of the amphitheatre to the northeast.

Descend from the col using the **fixed wires**, and then traverse over boulder slopes first north then east, climbing gradually over blocks to the obvious wooden marker post that indicates the start of the Galten Scharte. ▶

From the col proceed east along the ridge for a short distance to the Galten Scharte proper (2882m) (1hr). Good scenery hereabouts as the views open up, particularly of the Frosnitztal valley. Once at the Galten Scharte it becomes obvious why the route should only be undertaken in good weather. The route now descends very steep difficult ground for 1hr.

If you are in a group then **stay close together** to avoid dislodging rocks down onto each other and to provide assistance to your companions when necessary.

From the col descend the steep trail of sorts over loose shale, the upper sections of which are very exposed, with fixed ropes in places, continuing down zigzags until easier ground is reached at 2530m. **Do not stop here as the risk of stonefall is still very real.**

The slope now eases a little and continues northwest over a stone track and glacial debris at Frosnitzer Schafalm (or 'place to graze sheep'), to a **footbridge** and **signpost** on the Malfrosnitzbach. A further 5mins and another **signpost** is reached indicating the way to the Zedlacher Alm in the valley (a short 1hr). ▶

After the nervous demands of the Galten Scharte, what follows now is 1hr of very pleasant walking. Continue north, on Route 922, across the grassy slopes of the Galderet, with **fixed ropes** in place on the steep, difficult bits, to the **signpost** at the junction with the path coming up from the valley at **Steinsteg** (1hr). Continue as before northwest for a further half hour, now on Route 921, to the **signpost** at the junction with paths from the east. The hut is now visible, perched high above on its rocky promontory.

> Look out for the interesting rock features hereabouts on the Maurer Rote.

> This is a good place to stop for a break as you are now a little over half way to the Badener Hut.

Rock features at the Maurer Rote

From here the route cranks up several degrees to make the necessary 300m or more of ascent, first heading north along a good trail to the **footbridge** over the raging torrents coming off the Frosnitz Kees glacier, then turning west climbing through longish zigzags up the moraines of the Inderer Keesrugg for the final pull up to the hut (1hr).

Alternative Route
Should you be unfortunate enough when you reach the Bonn Matreier Hut to have bad weather making the crossing of the Galten Scharte inadvisable the following is offered as an alternative.

STAGE 4 – BONN MATREIER HUT TO BADENER HUT

Before setting out arrange for Venediger Taxis (04877 5369/5231) to meet you at the car park below Bodenalm at Trog then either to drop you off in Matrei from where you can get the bus either to Matreier Tauern Haus and then walk to Venediger Haus, or continue on the bus all the way to Venediger Haus.

From the hut retrace your steps on Route 922 to the first signpost, then take the left fork all the way down the Nilltal valley to the Nilljoch Hut.

At the hut turn right, west, and follow the forest track to the car park at Trog to meet up with Venediger taxis. See the hut directory for details of Venediger Haus.

From Venediger Haus you can continue along the Venediger Rucksack Route, having a choice of either the Neue Prager Hut or Sankt Poltener Hut as your next objective.

The Galten Scharte is not particularly difficult and no harder than crossing the Zopat Scharte in Stage 3, except that the difficulties are much more sustained.

It goes without saying that the Galten Scharte should only be undertaken in good weather. The reasons for this are basically twofold. Firstly the upper sections which you are to descend are very steep and very exposed and while they are provided with fixed wire ropes great care needs to be exercised as the consequences of a slip or fall are likely to be serious. Secondly, because the upper slopes are not very stable after rain they tend to run with water making the risk of stonefall very real. An added risk is that because the fixed wires follow the path of sorts it also acts as a lightning conductor which is not a good idea if you happen to be holding on to it in a thunder storm. And because the route is quite long and filled with uncertainty it makes sense to be on your way early.

STAGE 5
*Badener Hut to Neue Prager Hut
via the Loebbentorl*

Standard time	4–6hrs
Distance	7km
Ascent	About 700m

In terms of scenery this is perhaps the best day of the Rucksack Route and Venediger Hoehenweg as the scenery is simply stunning.

The early stages of the day are dominated by views down the Frosnitztal valley and peaks of the Wildenkogl that gradually hems us in to restrict the overall panorama, that is until the Loebbentorl with its instant 'wow' factor is reached. One moment you are beginning to feel hemmed in and claustrophobic and the next moment you are looking at the very best the Venediger can offer, with the high peaks of the Gross Venediger all set in the great glacial sea of the Schlaten Kees glacier with its jumbled mass of ice formations, huge crevasses and tumbling ice falls.

Even during the descent onto the foot of the Keesboden glacier the scenery is simply stunning. Once down and onto the glacier just trying to take in the scale of the Schlaten Kees ice fall that looms high above invokes a sense of high mountain grandeur, one to savour for just the few short minutes it takes to cross the glacier.

In the last hour between the Alte and Neue Prager Huts the scenery continues to enthral, with alternative views across the Schlaten Kees glacier and a quartet of peaks, Kristallwand, Hoher Zaun, Schwarze Wand and Rainer Horn leading to the Gross Venediger: reason enough to remember why this area was so important to those early pioneers Johann Studl and his friends from the OeAV Prague Sektion, who helped to make it all possible. A fitting way to end a very special day in the mountains.

From the back of the hut pick up the trail of Route 921 and the Venediger Hoehenweg.

Proceed northwest on a good path contouring around the hillside of the Kessboelach to a point at 2620m with

Stage 5 – Badener Hut to Neue Prager Hut

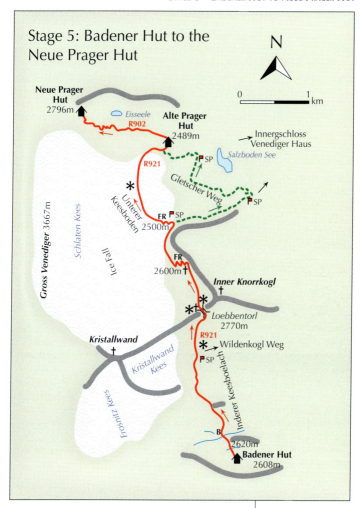

a rickety footbridge across the meltwaters coming off the Frosnitz Kees glacier. **Be careful with this section as snow tends to linger in the gullies well into the season.**

> There is excellent scenery on this section.

Continue as before to traverse across the hillside, now more broken and rocky, to the **signpost** at the junction of paths for the Wildenkogl Weg that heads across the Wildenkogl (3022m) to Matrei in Ost Tyrol. ◄

The *Loebbentorl* pass now lies immediately to the north. Proceed north on Route 921 over rocks and boulders for the 150m of ascent to the col, first gradually then more steeply to the Loebbentorl (2770m) with its huge crucifix playing host to one of the most iconic views in the Venediger, overlooking the Schlaten Kees glacier headed by the Gross Venediger (3660m) (1½hrs). It should come as no surprise that this was the location chosen by the DAV Baden *Sektion* to erect the cross as a memorial to their members who died in the two world wars.

> At the Loebbentorl overlooking the Schlaten Kees glacier with the Gross Venediger in the clouds, centre and Schwarze Wand Black Wall

From the col continue north on Route 921, descending the rocky flank of the Innerer Knorrkogl to the 2600m contour, where the route turns west to descend a series of zigzags over rocks and boulders to gain the glacial moraines proper at 2500m. This slope can be problematic as it is prone to retaining snow well into August. **Fixed wires** are in place to aid stability. The scenery here is outstanding with both the Alte and Neue Prager Huts clearly in view across the void to the north.

Stage 5 – Badener Hut to Neue Prager Hut

Follow the rocky trail as before to the **signpost** at the junction of the track leading down to the foot of the Keesboden glacier (1hr).

If the weather is good and there are no warning signs to say otherwise the preferred route to follow is down the moraine and across the glacier since in simple arithmetic terms it will save 1hr journey time, is shorter by two kilometres and will save 300m of descent/ascent. If the weather is none too good, with limited visibility, then take the long way round by continuing to descend the glacial moraines and follow first the *Rudolf Zoellner Weg* then **signs** for the OeAV Gletscherweg to the Alte Prager Hut.

Presuming good weather: from the signpost proceed west down steep zigzags over blocks and boulders and other general glacier debris for 100m or so to get on the glacier. The glacier is normally strewn with stones and grit which negates the need for crampons.

Proceed across the flattish section of the Unterer Keesboden glacier, first westerly then, turning north, look for marker posts and head for the obvious footpath coming down from the **Alte Prager Hut**. Get onto the path to make the 20mins of ascent to the Alte Prager Hut (1hr). ▶

From the Alte Prager Hut the Neue Prager Hut is 300m higher and about 1hr away.

From the Alte Prager Hut proceed west, now on Route 902, following a well-marked rocky trail, ascending first gradually then as the trail nears the hut climbing more steeply through a series of zigzags over rock slabs and block boulders to the hut (1hr).

Once again the scenery hereabouts is in the premier league.

While a relatively straightforward day's outing on well marked trails, the disadvantage of this stage is that it is a route you have to commit to, since there are no alternative routes should a mishap occur or the weather suddenly changes. Once committed you must cross the Loebbentorl or make the return journey to the comfort of the Badener Hut. ▶

The only other place where a decision has to be made is the junction with the path leading onto the foot of the Keesboden glacier.

If you are carrying full mountaineering gear this will present no difficulty whatsoever. However, if you are purely walkers, a decision will have to be made whether to progress across the foot of the glacier or to take the long way round via the OeAV Gletcherweg. Remember that in good settled weather the glacier will present no difficulty unless something has happened to it in which case signs of it being 'Gesprutt' (closed) will be evident, but only you can decide. If on the other hand the weather is changing and visibility is poor, the correct decision is to follow the safer route and take the long way round.

EXCURSION FROM NEUE PRAGER HUT

5.1 Ascent of the Gross Venediger (3660m)

See the Venediger Glacier Tour Stage 7 route description (page 116) for climbing the Gross Venediger.

Gross Venediger from Ostlicher Simony Spitz

STAGE 5A

*Badener Hut to Venediger Haus
(alternative bad weather route)*

Standard time	4hrs to Gruben
Distance	About 10km
Ascent	Nil

Should you be unfortunate enough to have bad weather at the Badener Hut making the crossing of the Loebbentorl to the Neue Prager Hut difficult then the following route will put you back on track, albeit a day late.

Retrace your steps back down the moraine slopes of the Inderer Keesrugg ridge to the signpost which gives two directions to Gruben. Take the right hand fork and once again cross the footbridge over the raging torrents of the Inderer Keesbach.

Continue for a short kilometre southeast to a signpost and junction with the path leading to the Galten Scharte. Take the left branch and on past the tiny alpine lake of Achselsee to the junction of paths with the main service road at Steinsteg.

Follow this service road down the valley for the next 3hrs past the small farmsteads at Mitteldorfer Alm and Katal Alm to the hamlet of Gruben.

At Gruben telephone Venediger Haus (0043 (0) 4875 8820) for their taxi service. Allow ½hr for them to turn up.

Once at Venediger Haus you are now in the right valley to continue with the Venediger Hoehenweg and the Rucksack Route and make your way to the Neue Prager Hut and or Sankt Poltener Hut.

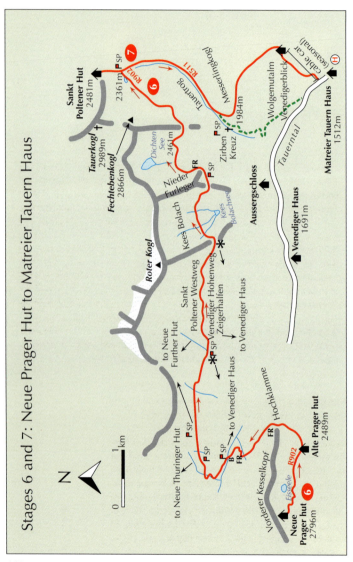

STAGE 6
Neue Prager Hut to Sankt Poltener Hut

Standard time	7hrs
Distance	14+km
Ascent	About 600m but a lot of up and down

The route has the distinction of being the longest on the Venediger Rucksack Route and Venediger Hoehenweg but perhaps more poignantly it marks the end of the journey across the Venediger. Despite this being the penultimate promenade on the Venediger Rucksack Route and Venediger Hoehenweg, this is a fine long-distance trail in its own right. Unfortunately and sadly the route starts to take us away from the heart of the Venediger.

This is a fine route that starts off easy, first backtracking downhill to the **Alte Prager Hut**, with splendid views of the Schwarze Wand and adjacent peaks, then a little mountaineering challenge to contour around the bulk of the Kesselkopf. This is then followed by first-class alpine walking that traverses high above Venediger Haus and the Tauerntal valley. It is around the area of the Roter Kogl that the true scale of the Gross Venediger with its attendant glaciers can be seen. Then finally, as the Venediger fades into the horizon and the Granat Group beckons, the splendid Sankt Poltener Hut is reached, marking a fitting way to end the Venediger Rucksack Route and Venediger Hoehenweg.

From the hut, retrace your steps on the now familiar Route 902 to the **signpost** at the Alte Prager Hut (20mins).

At the Alte Prager Hut, continue on Route 902 on the Venediger Hoehenweg heading northeast over broken ground on the 2500m contour to get around the huge rock buttress of the Vorderer Kesselkopf, with **fixed wires** in place at the **Hochklamme** gully. Follow the track, crossing several streams, to its natural end at the head of a second gully. Cross the stream and descend a series of zigzags over steep difficult ground, **fixed wires** again in place, to the **signpost** at the junction of paths coming up the valley from Venediger Haus (1½hrs).

Unseasonal July weather for OeAV member Stuart Pike

Cross the **bridge** to get over the raging torrents of the Viltragenbach, then head northwest then north through glacial debris, zigzagging to and fro for 300m to the junction of paths and a **signpost** indicating the way to the Neue Thuringer Hut (A short 1hr).

Continue over broken ground as before, but now in an easterly direction crossing a number of streams enroute to a second **signpost** that indicates the way to the Neue Further Hut. A little over a kilometre away a **signpost** at another junction of paths is reached at Zeigerhalfen (2506m), with paths heading up across the mountain to the Neue Further Hut and down the mountain to Venediger Haus and Innergschloss (1hr).

From here for the next few hours the route embraces excellent alpine walking, traversing the mountainside high above the valley roughly on the 2500m contour and crossing three distinct ridges.

Proceed to navigate through rocks and boulders to the first rocky spur coming down from the Roter Kogl. ◄

This is an excellent place for a rest stop, with first-class retrospective views toward the Gross Venediger and attendant glacier system.

Traverse around the Keesbolach couloir over boulders and broken ground crossing many streams that cross the area to the second obvious ridge at Niederer Furleger (2514m) and a **signpost** at a junction of paths leading

Stage 6 – Neue Prager Hut to Sankt Poltener Hut

down the mountain to the hamlet of Aussergschloss (a short 1hr).

Descend steep difficult ground, with **fixed ropes**, and traverse around the Dichtenkar couloir, now sharing the route with the Sankt Poltener Westweg, to the third ridge at the southern tip of the Fechtebenkogl's south ridge (¾hr). ▶

Round the ridge and follow the track northeast over rocks and boulders, paved in places, passing the tiny alpine lake at 2361m, to the **signpost** at the junction of paths coming from Aussergschloss (1hr).

For the short distance of what remains of the day's promenade, head north, zigzagging through the boulders to the hut with its famous Falber Tauern bell.

There are good views from here to the south in the direction of the Tauerntal valley.

The main challenge of the route is that it is quite long, by far the longest on the Venediger Rucksack Route and Venediger Hoehenweg, which means it is best avoided in poor weather. Despite the length of the journey there are few serious obstacles that have not been dealt with before in the crossing of the Venediger.

The first mountaineering challenge of the day is negotiating the steep sections around the Vorderer Kesselkopf buttress. Care needs to be exercised here as there are many streams that run off the Kesselkopf and the gullies are prone to retaining snow late into the season. After that, the middle section has quite a few boulder fields to navigate, where route markers are not always obvious; these are more problematic in mist or when snow covered.

Because of the distance, walkers are advised to be on their way early.

STAGE 7
Sankt Poltener Hut to Matreier Tauern Haus

Standard time	3hrs
Distance	6km
Ascent	Nil

A pleasant short walk that brings to an end the Venediger Rucksack Route and Venediger Hoehenweg.

The Hohe Tauern National Park minibus service to Matrei from Tauern Haus leaves at 10:10 and 13:10hrs.

From the hut, proceed south retracing your steps through the boulder field for 500m as far as the **signpost** above the small alpine tarn, Eisee. Take the left-hand branch continuing south on Route 511 generally following the line of a set of overhead electrical power lines and pylons, down through the open combe of Tauertrog, following the stony track adjacent to the Tauernbach stream. **Signpost** (1hr).

Here you have a choice of routes: if the weather is good, take the left-hand track southwest for 1km on a good track until the track turns east then southeast, contouring around the the southern flank of Messelingkogl on the 2000m contour to the top of the seasonal chair lift at Venedigerblick (1982m) (1hr). If the cable car is running (seasonal), make use of it, if not follow the signposted track southwest, down through the forest, to Matreier Tauern Haus.

Alternatively, if the weather is poor, continue south on Route 511 to the picnic spot at Zirbenkreuz (1984m), where there is a **signpost**, then descend through the forest to Wolgemutalm and pick up the graded track to Matreier Tauern Haus.

THE VENEDIGER GLACIER TOUR

ROUTE SUMMARY

		Standard time (hrs)	Distance (km)	Ascent (m)
1	Mayrhofen to Warnsdorfer Hut	3–4	6+	700
2	Warnsdorfer Hut to Essener Rostocker Hut	5	7	768
	Excursions from Essener Rostocker Hut			
	2.1 Ascent of the Drei Herrn Spitz	5–6+	4	1291
	2.2 Ascent of the Gross Geiger	5	5	1152
	2.3 Ascent of the Rostocker Eck	1½	1½	541
	2.4 Simonysee	1	1	180
	2.5 Ascent of Ostlicher Simony Spitz	4–5	3	1280
3	Essener Rostocker Hut to Johannis Hut	4	4	670
4	Johannis Hut to Bonn Matreier Hut	7	8	1100
5	Bonn Matreier Hut to Badener Hut	5–6	7	600
6	Badener Hut to Neue Prager Hut	4–6	7	>700
7	Neue Prager Hut to Kursinger Hut	7	10	870
	Excursion from Kursinger Hut			
	7.1 Ascent of the Keeskogl	2–3	>2	744
8.	Kursinger Hut to Warnsdorfer Hut	8	>7	900

This tour of eight continuous days is better suited to aspiring mountaineers for, as the name suggests, the tour takes in the very best of the Venediger, traversing the range on the inner circle in an anti-clockwise direction starting at the Warnsdorfer Hut then to each of the following huts: Essener-Rostocker, Johannis, Bonn Matreier, Badener, Neue Prager, Kursinger and back to the Warndorfer to close the circle. There is ample opportunity to climb several of the local peaks along the way.

This is a superb mountaineering tour and well worth the effort!

Getting there and back

From Innsbruck by train to Jenbach followed by the regional narrow-gauge railway, the Zillertalbahn, for the 1hr journey to the resort town of Mayrhofen then local bus service to Krimml, followed by a taxi to get you as far as the Krimml Tauern Haus.

There is a regional train service from Innsbruck which links up with the Zillertalbahn train service to Mayrhofen running throughout the week. Thereafter the local bus service from Mayrhofen to Krimml leaves at 08.30hrs, and takes a short hour to link up with various minibus taxi services including that operated by Krimmler Tauern Haus, leaving Krimml at 08:45/10:30hrs. From Krimml various other taxi services are available to Krimmler Tauern Haus: tel 06465 8327.

The return transport details are naturally the same in reverse. From Krimmler Tauern Haus by minibus taxi service, operated by the hotel, to Krimml, then the post bus to Mayrhofen followed by trains to Jenbach and Innsbruck. Minibuses from Krimmler Tauern Haus to Krimml are at 08.00/09.30/10.00/15.30/17.00hrs.

STAGE 1

Mayrhofen to Warnsdorfer Hut

Standard time	3–4hrs
Distance	>6km
Ascent	700m

See approach notes above for transport details. Take the local bus service from Mayrhofen to the small town of Krimml, journey time about 1hr.

From Krimml the Krimmler Tauern Haus is 9km or 5hrs. It is strongly recommended that you get a taxi from the town square in Krimml or make use of the minibus service operated by Krimml Tauern Haus to get you as far as the Krimmler Tauern Haus itself.

From the very touristy Krimmler Tauern Haus (1622m) follow the graded single track road through the pleasant Krimmler Achental valley, following Routes 519–902. The first 3km is dominated by picturesque alpine scenery of forest and meadows, passing through several small farms on the way.

Turning the corner at Inn Anlas Alm the valley opens up to the mountains to reveal the glacial mass of the Krimmler Kees on the Drei Herrn Spitz (3498m), now sadly only half the mass it was in 1900.

After 1½hrs of road walking the graded track ends at *Innere Keesalm* 1804m, from where the real work begins to ascend the 600m to the hut. From the road head follow the obvious trail over rocks and zigzags to the hut (1½hrs).

STAGE 2

Warnsdorfer Hut to Essener Rostocker Hut via the Gams Spitzl and Maurertorl

Standard time	5hrs
Distance	7km
Ascent	768m

A splendid glacier promenade among the high peaks. This is the first of the major glacier crossings on the Glacier Tour, providing a very good introduction of things to come and in many ways sets the standard for the tour.

Trekking in Austria's Hohe Tauern

The initial part of the route to the Gams Spitzl, while hard going, is scenically varied with the big mountains of the Simony Spitz and Drei Herrn Spitz taking centre stage but also carpets of vivid blue Spring Gentian should help to take your mind momentarily away from carrying a big bag.

Once on the Gams Spitzl the peaks open up to a sea of glaciers giving the promenade its 'wow' factor, which should continue to enthral any climber all the way to the Maurertorl, the high point of the day at 3108m.

Thereafter, the descent to the hut through the glacier will provide a mountaineering challenge to round off the day.

From the hut proceed east on Route 902, which starts off immediately uphill, passing a **signpost** for the Gams Spitzl. Be careful not to get on the wrong track which leads off to the right, southeast, to the local beauty spot at Eissee.

The route follows more or less the rocky ridge zig-zagging to and fro for the next 1½hrs until the ridge is crossed, when the little satellite peak of Gams Spitzl is reached complete with metal cross, opening up a wonderful sea of glaciers (1½–2hrs). ◄

The way ahead to the Maurertorl is hidden from view at this stage but take time to look across the void toward the Venediger Scharte that will be descended during the days ahead.

Tackle up, get onto the Obersulzbach Kees glacier and head in an easterly direction on a rocky ridge which obscures the view up the glacier. Head for the low part of the ridge and cross it roughly on the 2850m contour. From here the Maurertorl is clearly visible. Continue to climb diagonally right to left avoiding, crevasses midway, to the col (1½hrs).

Excellent views back down the Obersulzbach Kees glacier and the adjacent peak, the Gross Geiger. Those with good eyesight will see the Kursinger Hut from the col, then the Essener Rostocker Hut while descending through the glacier.

STAGE 2 – WARNSDORFER HUT TO ESSENER ROSTOCKER HUT

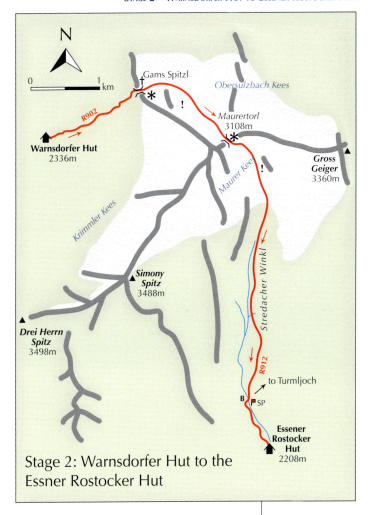

From the col the route descends very steeply dropping 600m in 2km. Global warming is taking its toll on the upper part of the Maurer Kees glacier. From the col proceed southeast in the direction of the Gross Geiger and the lower rocks of the Maurerkeeskopf, descending through the glacier for about 100m (10mins), when a bank of crevasses will become obvious at around 3000m.

Negotiate the crevasses and then proceed south. The traditional route as shown on the OeAV map, went straight down the glacier. More recently because of hard ice a more circuitous route was undertaken on the left bank, heading east until the ground became more forgiving, picking up the traditional waymarked route through rocks and boulders around 2700m. (1hr+).

Continue more leisurely, following a well-defined path along the Stredacher Winkl valley floor to the hut (1hr).

> The main difficulties of the day are on the southern side of the Maurertorl, as the glacier becomes more problematic. With good snow cover it can be very straightforward. However with minimal snow cover the lower section can be very scrappy, being a mix of hard ice and broken difficult ground which will demand care.

EXCURSIONS FROM ESSENER ROSTOCKER HUT

The Essener Rostocker Hut is one of the best huts for climbers, ideally placed for excursions along the Austrian–Italian border as well as forays onto local peaks. Before deciding what to climb enquire at the hut about which peaks are in good condition.

2.1 Ascent of the Drei Herrn Spitz

Standard time	>5–6hrs
Distance	4km
Ascent	1291m
Grade	PD+ (III)

This is the premiere peak of the region and one of the hardest to climb. The approach is quite long and involves considerable glacier work.

Standard time is forecast at 5–6hrs but you should allow 1–2hrs more due to the unpredictable nature of the Umbal Kees glacier, the top end of which is guarded by some gigantic crevasses.

From the hut proceed west along Route 902 to the signpost for Reggentorl. Proceed to the col negotiating rocks and boulders which blocked the col from a landslide in 2005 (2–2½hrs).

Get onto the Umbal Kees glacier and traverse north to a point at 3215m under Hinterer Gubach Spitz. Now traverse due west through the very heart of the glacier with its cavernous crevasses to the foot of the south ridge to meet the route coming from the Birnlucken Hut (2+hrs).

Get onto the ridge by climbing to the left of a rocky rib, then follow the snow arête to the summit (1hr).

2.2 Ascent of the Gross Geiger

Standard time	5hrs
Distance	5km
Ascent	1152m
Grade	F+ (I–II)

From the hut proceed north up the valley following signposts for the Johannis Hut. After the footbridge

TREKKING IN AUSTRIA'S HOHE TAUERN

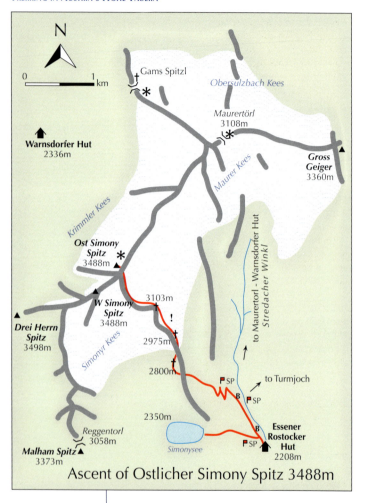

Ascent of Ostlicher Simony Spitz 3488m

over the Maurer Bach the path climbs steadily heading for the Turmljoch (2790m) (1hr). along this track a signpost indicates the way to the Gross Geiger. The original route climbed the ridge of the Grosses Hap 3350m but this has lost some favour in recent years to an alternative route going around it. Make for a point on the ridge at 2904m, then traverse the snow slopes more or less level to a point on the next ridge at 2983m. Round the foot of the ridge and head for the top of the col at a point 3219m. Thereafter scramble southeast up the ridge to the summit.

2.3 Ascent of the Rostocker Eck

Standard time	1½hrs
Distance	1½km
Ascent	541m

A steep but well marked easy path leads up, over and around this delightful little peak with excellent scenery. 1½hrs, up to 3–4hrs for the round trip.

2.4 Simonysee (2350m)

Standard time	1hr
Distance	1km
Ascent	180m

Glacial lake at the foot of the Simony Kees glacier. Good picnic spot.

2.5 Ascent of Ostlicher Simony Spitz

Standard time	4–5hrs
Distance	3km
Ascent	1280m
Grade	PD+ (III)

A worthy excursion up one of the most popular mountains in the region.

From the hut ignore the immediate signs and proceed up the Stredacher valley, over the footbridge, on past a sign for Simonysee, then a little further a signpost is reached indicating the way up the mountain (20mins).

The path now heads west on a good path and climbs quickly up the hillside of Dellache Keesflecke via a series of steep zigzags to 2800m (1hr).

Thereafter the path of sorts deteriorates into many false trails, with stone cairns in places but not consistently, to climb a vague ridge of rocks, boulders, patches of snow and sections of scrappy ground (1hr).

At the 3000m mark the ridge becomes more defined as it abuts the start of the upper snow fields at 3103m. Continue to climb the ridge over very steep exposed broken ground, boulders and blocks until the ridge becomes too steep to climb and forces you right onto the snow (1hr).

Get onto the snow and climb the steep but obvious slope to around 3200m where you will have to decide

Ascent of Ostlicher Simony Spitz

whether to keep your crampons on to negotiate the next series of rocks or take them off (1hr).

Finally climb the last snow slope of the Simony Kees glacier, very steep at the top, to emerge on the knife-edged summit crest with impressive views in all directions (1hr). This is an excellent day out up a popular mountain.

In terms of mountaineering the challenges are in the upper half both on rock and in negotiating the relatively steep snow slopes which will provide the necessary interest to justify its grade.

THE VIEW FROM OSTLICHER SIMONY SPITZ

The views from the top are extensive particularly to the north where those with good eyesight will be able to locate the Warnsdorfer Hut and adjacent Eissee and in the far distance the conical shape of the Reichen Spitze. Closer to hand is the intimidating knife edge arête leading to the Westlicher Simony Spitz, the traverse to which is way beyond the scope of these notes. Finally to the east are the local peaks of the Gross Venediger and its close companion the Gross Geiger then back down the Stredacher valley toward the Essener Rostocker Hut and Drei Herrn Spitz.

The main difficulties on this ascent are midway on the route when negotiating the steep broken ground which is loose and scrappy and not well marked, and again when getting on and off rocks onto the snow slopes which are steep and exposed. The good news is that the route finding is marginally easier in descent. Obviously these difficulties would be exacerbated with cloud cover.

WESTLICHER SIMONY SPITZ

The ascent of Westlicher Simony Spitz is too serious a route to be covered in these notes.

STAGES 3–6

For these (Essener Rostocker Hut to Johannis Hut, Johannis Hut to Bonn Matreier Hut, Bonn Matreier Hut to Badener Hut and Badener Hut to Neue Prager Hut) see the route descriptions for the Venediger Rucksack Route, Stages 2–5, page 82.

STAGE 7

Neue Prager Hut to Kursinger Hut via the Gross Venediger

Standard time	7hrs
Distance	10km
Ascent	870m

The premiere stage of the Venediger Glacier Tour, full of scenic interest and mountaineering challenge. Enjoy.

From the hut, proceed west following the well marked trail through the rocks and boulders of the Niederer Zaun to the weather station on the 3000m contour for a short 1hr.

Tackle up and get onto the Schlaten Kees glacier. Cross the glacier in a southwesterly direction generally aiming for a notch in the ridge between the Hoehes Adlerl and Gross Venediger, progressing through a bank of crevasses for approximately 1km and negotiating a distinct step around 3200m (1hr). ◄

The view across the Schlaten Kees ice fall toward the Schwarze Wand is superb.

Once through the crevasse zone, proceed toward the centre of the glacier to a point south of the Kleine Venediger and Venediger Scharte, defining the route to the Kursinger Hut.

Continue as before up the glacier, but now heading west to join the Gross Venediger's south ridge anywhere

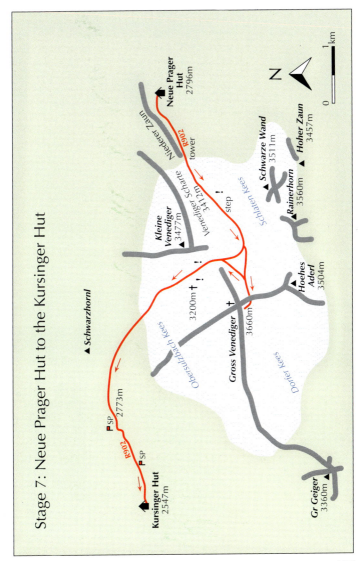

between the 3500m and 3600m contours. Kit may be stashed midway to make a semi-lightweight ascent of the mountain without the need to carry the whole contents of a rucksack.

Once on the ridge, the exposure becomes much greater with the north side of the mountain dropping away fearsomely fast. Be careful hereabouts as in summer the mountain is congested with climbers vying for the mountain's attention.

Proceed up the ridge that gradually steepens and narrows then levels out at the top; immediately thereafter traverse the level summit ridge for around 100m to the ornate summit cross. Excellent views in all directions (2hrs).

In descent, for those returning to the Neue Prager Hut return by the same route paying particular attention to the step in the glacier which is harder to negotiate in descent than ascent.

On the Gross Venediger summit ridge

Stage 7 – Neue Prager Hut to Kursinger Hut

THE GROSS VENEDIGER

The question of the true height of the Gross Venediger will always remain since the mountain is a true snow peak with no rock on the summit. Reviewing several maps and publications, the mountains height is given as 3660, 3666, 3667, 3674m; the height given in this guide book is that indicated on the latest edition of the OeAV map, 3660m. The Gross Venediger is a big mountain at 3660m, being the fourth highest in Austria after the Gross Glockner, Otztal Wild Spitze and Weisskogel respectively.

For a big mountain it is also one of the easiest to climb with few sustained objective dangers; this means it is very popular in summer to all manner of folk wanting to bag a mountain of substance.

Having said that, the Gross Venediger is a fine mountain, a true snow peak that has the most connected glacier system in the Eastern Alps. The route itself is studded with scenic gems with the glacier scenery being special and stunning particularly in ascent with the view across the Schlatten Kees glacier and its complex ice fall to the peaks of the Schwarze Wand (3511m), the Black Wall, and Rainerhorn (3560m) named after a famous military Field Marshall and Royal family member of the Hapsburg dynasty.

Once on the summit the views are in the true sense of the word panoramic, with close neighbours dominating the scene particularly the Gross Geiger (3360m), that is particularly fine, then further afield to Drei Herrn Spitz (3499m) and Ostliches Simony Spitz (3488m) which was climbed earlier on the Glacier Tour. Then, around to the east and across the void is the unmistakable outline of the Gross Glockner (3798m) and the bulk of the Weissbachhorn (3564m), while those with exception eyesight will be able to locate the mini-Matterhorn of the region, the Reichen Spitze (3303m) and far below it the Kursinger Hut.

For those heading for the Kursinger Hut, return to collect your stash of gear then head northeast to the Venediger Scharte (3413m) and proceed down through the *scharte*, descending increasingly steepening slopes and an awkward step down on the 3300m contour through a series of crevasses.

Continue now more northerly down through the natural basin of the Obersulzbach Kees glacier to a point where the ice fall begins to drop away. Hereabouts turn and head northwest for a short 2km making for a point to

Descending from the Venediger Scharte

exit the glacier below the Schwarzhornl (3099m) and the head of the Obersulzbach Kees ice fall.

Get off the glacier and pick up the familiar trail of Route 902 through rocks and boulders to the collection of buildings that form the Kursinger Hut.

This is a big route on a big mountain that will demand route finding and mountaineering skills not to mention being hindered by the effects of altitude and being out of puff.

The main challenge of the route is route finding. The Gross Venediger is not a mountain to undertake on a falling barometer and one to definitely avoid when covered in mist due to the propensity for white-out conditions.

As for mountaineering difficulty there are three areas that will demand care, the first being the prominent step where the Schlaten Kees glacier suddenly steepens through a group of crevasses. The second is the summit ridge which is very exposed and made more difficult because of the numbers of climbers on the mountain creating situations that add unnecessary risk. Lastly, at the glacier step at the head of the Obersulzbach Kees glacier just below the Venediger Scharte the threat of crevasses is very real and a fall would be difficult to stop.

EXCURSION FROM KURSINGER HUT

7.1 Ascent of the Keeskogel (3291m)

Standard time	2½hrs
Distance	2+km
Ascent	744m

See map on page 123

A pleasant half day outing with excellent panoramic views.

The route is characterised by three distinct sections. From the hut the first section proceeds northeast on a good but not always well marked rocky trail to a point at 2800m. The middle section continues north more steeply, toing and froing over slabby rocks and boulders with route markers deteriorating and not always obvious. The last section climbs the southwest ridge over very steep and loose difficult ground with odd sections protected by **fixed wires** that are not much use and onto the summit with its metal cross. ▶

Despite the unpleasant looseness of the rock this is not a bad route.

The views from the top are extensive but if you come away with any lasting memories it will be of the Gross Geiger (3360m).

TREKKING IN AUSTRIA'S HOHE TAUERN

The Gross Venediger from the Keeskogel

The only word of warning is when negotiating the upper summit rocks: not only are they very steep they are also very loose and pose a very real risk of participants showering other individuals with rocks, as the author can testify.

STAGE 8
Kursinger Hut to Warnsdorfer Hut via the Obersulzbach Kees Glacier and Gams Spitzl

Standard time	8hrs (but see clarification below)
Distance	7+km
Ascent	900m

STAGE 8 – KURSINGER HUT TO WARNSDORFER HUT

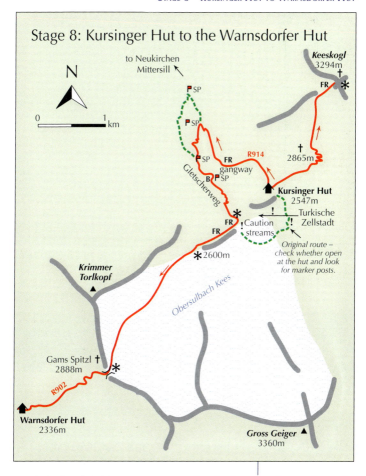

An excellent day out full of challenge in a big mountain environment.

The standard time quoted in official sources is woefully inadequate and while I have estimated 8hrs you should allow all day as everything rests on the state of the glacial streams and rivers at the foot of the Turkische

▶ Zellstadt and the condition of the Obersulzbach Kees glacier. The route described here will provide a safe if somewhat longer journey.

Although meltwater presents some serious difficulties the scenic content of the journey is superb, especially of the Gross Geiger (3360m) and the expanse of the Obersulzbach Kees glacier all the way around to the Gross Venediger. Then later as we retrace our footsteps from the Gams Spitzl the Drei Herrn Spitz comes back into view once again, and if you climbed the Ostlicher Simony Spitz (3488m) you will be able to reflect on and point to your past success.

From the hut proceed northwest on Route 914 heading down into the Obersulzbach valley, following the well-marked rocky trail through boulders, slabs and protected **gangways** to a vague junction of paths and **signpost** for the Warnsdorfer Hut. Follow this trail, vague in places, across grassy slopes strewn with boulders to a **footbridge** with a **signpost** indicating the path for the Gletscherweg (1+hrs).

The easy work over and now sadly 500m lower, follow this trail with its protected gangways southeast,

Stage 8 as seen from Kursinger Hut

STAGE 8 – KURSINGER HUT TO WARNSDORFER HUT

Below the Kursinger Hut with the Gross Geiger on the left, Maurertorl on the right

passing a sign which states that the Gletscherweg to the Kursinger Hut is 'gesprutt' and for experienced alpinists only until the trail comes to a natural conclusion at the Turkische Zellstadt, translated as the 'Turkish Encampment', named, no doubt, from some long-forgotten encounter between the Ottoman and Hapsburg dynasties. The scenery now changes into pure raw nature as the foot of the Obersulzbach Kees glacier is reached with ice pools, gaping chasms and raging rivers complemented with fabulous views of the Gross Geiger (1+hrs).

The foot of the glacier is usually sufficiently strewn with rocks and grit to make walking possible without the aid of crampons for the couple of hundred metres to the foot of an obvious ridge to the right at the convergence of several glacial streams/rivers.

Take time to look for the usual red and white route markers through the meltwater before continuing, and make sure all participants are clear as to what will be expected of them as surefootedness will be needed to the full for the next hour or so.

Doug Ball trying to make sense of the signs at the Turkische Zell Stadt

Approach the meltwater head on and carefully follow the route markers up through the streams, generally trying to follow the crest of the ridge. ◄ Avoid the temptation to go to the sides when the ground seems easier as a number of streams peel off into raging white water at the edges. If you are in a group keep close together providing assistance to each other and making good use of those trekking poles.

As with water anywhere in mountains approach with extreme caution, this is not a place for a fall or for dithering.

After 100m or so of white water excitement the path of sorts eases out to climb a section of **fixed wires** before getting onto the ridge proper (1hr).

Climb the steep rocky ridge over boulders and broken ground to emerge at a little col at 2600m on the left bank of the Obersulzbach Kees glacier, with the Gams Spitzl (2888m) clearly in view to the southwest (1½–2hrs).

STAGE 8 – KURSINGER HUT TO WARNSDORFER HUT

Tackle up and get onto the glacier (hopefully it won't be furrowed like a ploughed field) and make a rising traverse keeping to the left bank, west, with minimal crevasse danger, to the little col at the left-hand side of the Gams Spitzl (1½hrs). Excellent glacier scenery hereabouts.

From the Gams Spitzl follow the trail southwest on Route 902, on the Central Alpine Way, to the Warnsdorfer Hut, enjoying fabulous views of the mile-long ridge which leads from the Simony Spitz to the Drei Herrn Spitz (3499m), to complete the Venediger Glacier Tour (1hr).

Before setting out enquire at the hut about the viability of the routes shown on the OeAV maps to the south which access the glacier via the area known as the Turkische Zellstadt. These are the old recognised routes between huts and will knock two hours off the route described here. Also check the routes out on the ground, looking for signposts which warn 'nur fur geubte, gefahlich, schweirig', meaning difficult and dangerous, or *gesprutt*, which means closed and unlikely to reopen. (The reason for this is the declining state of the glacier and a number of massive avalanches which have wiped out what path there was.)

On my last visit the route described here was partly marked by red and white marker poles but I cannot see these lasting, hence my description which errs on the side of caution. The real difficulty of the route is without doubt the glacial streams at the foot of the ridge just above the Turkische Zellstadt which have to be climbed. This is not a place you'd choose to have to traverse, and while fortunately short it does demand ultimate concentration; get it wrong and the force of water will knock you off your feet.

The only other consideration is that because of these difficulties it is obviously not a route to undertake in less than ideal weather. If the weather is poor and wet then the journey out through the Obersulzbach valley is long and tedious but safe.

THE GROSS GLOCKNER GROUP

Looking toward the Gross Glockner from the Blaues Schartl Kampl

INTRODUCTION AND TOPOGRAPHY

This group is the main centre of the Hohe Tauern National Park, inextricably linked to the Gross Glockner (3798m), the highest mountain in Austria and the focal point of the group.

The valleys which define the group are the Pinzgau in the north with the main towns of Kaprun, Zell am See and Uttendorf. The Fuschertal valley to the east links Kaprun in the north with Heiligenblut in the south, with the Amertal and Tauerntal to the west, dividing the group from the Venediger.

In addition to the Gross Glockner, there are around a dozen other glaciated peaks over 3000m and many other mountains over 3000m, with one or two that edge their way in from the Granat Group, easily accessible from the west. While not as heavily glaciated as the Venediger Group, the mountains around the Gross Glockner and around the central massif are heavily glaciated. The Pasterzen Kees glacier which complements the classic view of the Gross Glockner from Franz Josefs Haus retains the title of being the longest single glacier in Austria and the Eastern Alps.

Unlike the Venediger, where glaciers restrict freedom of movement through the mountains, the Glockner Group is quite the opposite, being linked with glacier-free cols and passes. It goes without saying that this is a first class group of mountains and worthy of a visit in its own right, even without climbing the Gross Glockner.

Hut-to-Hut Routes

As in my other Alpine trekking guidebooks, routes are named to indicate clearly the type of journey participants will undertake and what mountaineering skills will be required. The Rucksack Route requires no greater skills than those needed to wander the mountain areas of Britain safely.

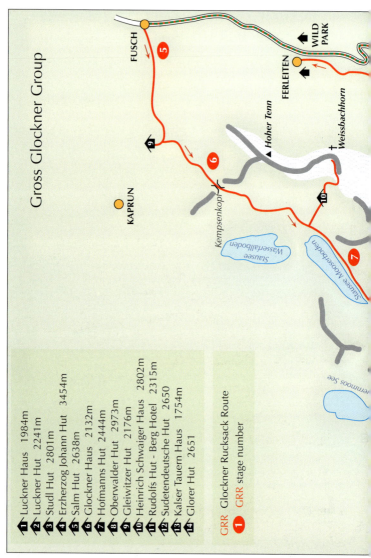

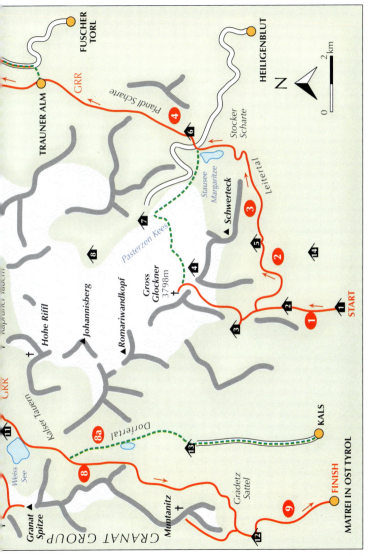

THE GLOCKNER GROUP
HUT-TO-HUT RUCKSACK ROUTE

Gross Glockner as seen from In der Multer

The Glockner *Runde Tour* (round tour) came about through a collaboration between the Hohe Tauern National Park Authority and the Austrian Alpine Club in 2002 to celebrate the 'Year of the Mountains'. The objective was to create a route around the Gross Glockner that would allow participants total freedom of movement through the mountains without having to make difficult glacier crossings and carry mountaineering equipment, ropes and what have you.

This route of eight continuous days, as described in this guide book, is, as the name suggests, a circular tour around Austria's highest mountain. The route starts at the Studl Hut then visits each of the following huts: Salm, Glockner Haus, the village of Fusch, Gleiwitzer, Heinrich Schwaiger Haus, Rudolfs Hut/Berg Hotel, to end at the Sudetendeutsche Hut or Kalser Tauern Haus, with opportunities to climb some of the local peaks along the way.

Having stated the obvious it is necessary to offer a few clarifications of how the guide has been constructed. The only reason for including the Studl Hut in the itinery is to climb the Gross Glockner. If the

The Glockner Group Hut-to-Hut Rucksack Route

ROUTE SUMMARY

		Standard time (hrs)	Distance (km)	Ascent (m)
1	Luckner Haus to Studl Hut	2½	4	820
	Excursions from Studl Hut			
	1.1 Ascent of the Gross Glockner	5+	2½	900
	1.2 Erzherzog Johann Hut to Glockner Haus via the Meletzkigrat (Alternative descent from the Gross Glockner)	6	11	200
	1.3 Ascent of the Romariswandkopf	5	4	740
2	Studl Hut to Salm Hut	2½–3	5	300
3	Salm Hut to Glockner Haus	2½–3	6	250
4	Glockner Haus to Fusch	6–7	12–19	550
5	Fusch to Gleiwitzer Hut	4	5+	1360
6	Gleiwitzer Hut to Heinrich Schwaiger Haus	8–10	8	1650
	Excursions from Heinrich Schwaiger Haus			
	6.1 Ascent of the Grosses Weisbachhorn	4	1+	760
6A	Gleiwitzer Hut to Kaprun			
7	Heinrich Schwaiger Haus to Rudolfs Hut/Berg Hotel	7–8	9	860
	Excursions from Rudolfs Hut			
	7.1 Ascent of the Stubacher Sonnblick and Granat Spitze	4–5	4	830
	7.2 Gletcher Panoramweg	3	4	200
8	Rudolfs Hut to Sudetendeutsche Hut	7–8	11	1050
	Excursions from Sudetendeutsche Hut			
	8.1 Ascent of the Grosser Muntanitz	2–3	3	600
8A	Rudolfs Hut to Kalser Tauern Haus	4	7	200
9	Sudetendeutsche Hut to Matrei in Ost Tyrol	3½–4	7	100

mountain is not on your agenda then there is no reason to go to the Studl Hut if you do not want to: you may wish to start the tour from the Salm Hut, and so save one day's walking.

Although information published by the National Park makes it clear you can start the *Runde Tour* anywhere, the guiding principle is that you start from Kaprun, then visit the following huts: Rudolfs, Sudetendeutsche or Kalser Tauern Haus, the village of Kals, then to the Salm Hut and Glockner Haus, across to the village of Fusch, and end at the tour at the Gleiwitzer Hut, thus avoiding the long journey between the Gleiwitzer Hut and Heinrich Schwaiger Haus. The main objective in visiting Heinrich Schwaiger Haus is to climb the Grosses Weisbachhorn.

The 'official' route is therefore more of a horseshoe tour than a circular one. The published information also has the disadvantage of having to make two journeys down into the valley, first the crossing from the Sudetendeutsche Hut or Kalser Tauern Haus to Kals or Matrei in Ost Tyrol to make the connection with the Salm Hut, the second being the hut connection between Glockner Haus and the village of Fusch.

Those who are not mountaineers but are experienced winter walkers of British or Nordic hills should seriously consider hiring a professional mountain guide for a few days at the start of the tour to enable the Gross Glockner (3798m) to be climbed. Whatever you decide this is a fine tour and you will not be disappointed.

Maps
- Austrian Alpine Club Alpenvwereinskarte *Grossglocknergruppe* sheet 40 1:25,000 scale.
- Kompass *Glocknergruppe* Nationalpark Hohe Tauern sheet 39. 1:50,000 scale.
- Freytag and Berndt *Grossglockner – Kaprun – Zell am See* sheet 122. 1:50,000 scale.

Getting there and back
Unfortunately there are no easy approaches to the Gross Glockner Group: most are a bit tedious unless you have your own transport and rely on trains and the local bus service, taking up much of the first day.

From Innsbruck or Salzburg, take the train to Kitzbuhel then the regional bus to Luckner Haus via Mittersill in the

Pinzgau valley and Matrei in Ost Tyrol and Huben, then finally Kals to Luckner Haus. The normal train service from Innsbruck throughout the week leaves at 09:25hrs, which linking up with the bus service from Kitzbuhel at 10:35hrs and arriving at Huben, via Matrei in Ost Tyrol, at 12:00hrs. Change bus at Huben and depart at 12:31hrs, arriving at Luckner Haus at 13:2hrs.

A taxi service is also available from Matrei in Ost Tyrol to Luckner Haus: call Venediger Taxis (tel 0043 (0) 4877 5369/5231).

If you plan to end the tour as described you need to be at the bus station in Matrei in Ost Tyrol opposite the Hotel Sport by 13:30hrs. The local bus service from Matrei (13.45hrs) arrives in Kitzbuhel at 15:03hrs. The train from Kitzbuhel (15:19hrs) arrives in Innsbruck at 16:26hrs.

STAGE 1
Luckner Haus to Studl Hut

Standard time	2½hrs
Ascent	820m
Distance	4km

A straightforward journey with no particular difficulties. Excellent scenery throughout being wholly dominated by the Gross Glockner 3798m which gets its name as it is said to resemble, when viewed from this direction, a bell, hence its name, the 'Big Bellringer'.

It goes without saying that the only real reason for making the journey to the Studl Hut is to climb the Gross Glockner, either by way of the normal route or the much harder Studl Grat.

From the hustle and bustle of the Luckner Haus, from where you can see the obvious Luckner Hut and the less obvious Erzherzog Johann Hut (Adlersruhe) high on the Gross Glockner, follow signs and Route 702 northwards

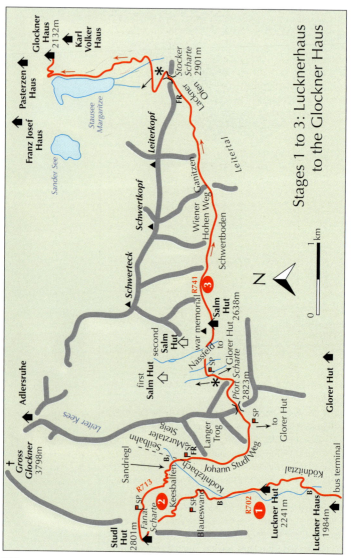

STAGE 1 – LUCKNER HAUS TO STUDL HUT

Gross Glockner from Luckner Haus

along the single track graded road through the last of the forest for a short hour to the Luckner Hut (2241m). ▶

Continue north as before, following the well marked rocky trail which changes from road to path where, after a few minutes, a signpost is reached indicating the route to the Glorer and Salm Huts, then 5mins later a single plank **bridge** is reached to cross the meltwaters of the Koednitzbach coming from the glaciers high above.

Hereafter the route picks up pace and zigzags up the steep slopes of the Blaues Wandle and junction of path to the Glorer and Salm Huts, signpost with warning notices

The scenery, especially across the Gross Glockner's southern slopes, is once again excellent.

that the route is for mountaineers only as the way across the Koenitzbach glacial river is *gesprutt*, dangerous and difficult.

Meanwhile our route now turns northwest climbing steadily over rocks and a well laid out paved staircase across the flank of the Blauewand to emerge eventually on the Fanat Scharte and Studl Hut (1hr).

EXCURSIONS FROM STUDL HUT

1.1 Ascent of the Gross Glockner

Standard time	2½–3hrs hut-to-hut plus 2½hrs to climb the mountain
Ascent	900m
Distance	2½km
Grade	PD+ (III)

If your intention is to climb the Gross Glockner then some strategy needs to be worked out as there are a couple of options open to you. It goes without saying that most people staying at the Studl Hut will be climbing on the Gross Glockner, either on the ordinary route or on the Studl Grat.

For those climbing the Studl Grat and those with limited time who wish to be up and down the mountain, the first call of the day is the dawn chorus at 4am. Since the Studl Grat is graded AD+ it is beyond the scope of these notes: the preferred option described here is to leave the Studl Hut at 0800hrs, make the journey to the Adlersruhe ('Eagles Rest'), have lunch, climb the mountain in the early afternoon and return to the Adlersruhe for an overnight stay. That way you will avoid the dawn rush from the Studl Hut and the crowds descending from the Adlersruhe.

For me the beauty of this route, coupled to staying overnight at the Erzherzog Johann Hut, is that it takes the heat out of the situation when the mountain is busy with people. I won't say you can climb the mountain in a leisurely style, just a better style when so many people are on the mountain. It is less stressful, safer and more enjoyable. This is a very good route and scenically stunning.

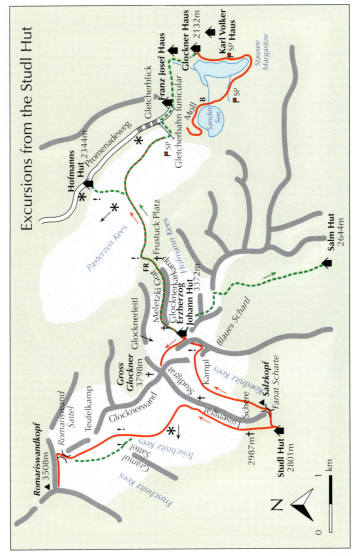

After the initial section the route soon opens out to provide an exceptional alpine promenade. The journey across the glacier is straightforward with very little crevasse danger: it allows participants to engage with the mountain as the foot of the south face is crossed. Thereafter good scrambling on sound rock adds to the experience as the route goes from strength to strength. Then what better than to have a proper lunch before continuing to tackle the more serious stuff which, although not hard in mountaineering terms, is challenging, with one or two very exposed situations leading up to the crux of the route through the Glockner Scharte and onto the summit with a 360° panorama across the whole of Austria. For such a big mountain this is a very pleasant route and if you are a seasoned scrambler and vertigo-free it is probably within your capability.

During the initial part of the journey the Gross Glockner is hidden from view by the foot of the Studl Grat and Salzkopf.

◀ From the Studl Hut retrace your steps the short distance to the Fanat Scharte with various signposts and stark warnings about the difficulty of the Studl Grat. Thereafter follow Route 712 over the rocky, shaley trail east, past the foot of the Luisengrat, named after Studl's wife Louise, and around the Salzkopf to arrive eventually in a huge combe below the south face of the Gross Glockner (½hr). Excellent situation with the Adlersruhe hut clearly in view perched on the distant ridge.

Tackle up and get onto the Koednitz Kees glacier, first heading north up to the magical 3000m contour before swinging right, east, under the south face, climbing the steepening snow slopes to the foot of an obvious ridge noted as 'Kampl' on the OeAV map.

This is a good safe place to de-tackle and stow your ice tools before continuing.

Get off the glacier, which is sometimes made awkward by a difficult step onto the rocks, and climb the rock buttress for a short distance with the aid of fixed ropes over steep ground to emerge on the ridge of the Blaues Schartl Kampl proper. ◀

The route from hereon is self evident and follows the ridge direct to the hut by scrambling over steep rocky terrain klettersteig/via ferrata-style, with lots of fixed wires and staples to aid your way up to the Adlersruhe.

From the hut climb the rocks immediately behind the hut to the upper reaches of the Hofmann Kees glacier

EXCURSIONS FROM STUDL HUT

Route up the Gross Glockner (dotted line shows where the route is behind the ridge from this viewpoint)

(15mins). Tackle up and climb the snow slopes in a northwesterly direction heading for the foot of the rock buttress, the Glocknerleitl, on the Klein Glockner marked by a tiny col (1hr). In good conditions most folks leave their axe and crampons hereabouts before continuing. Unless there is cloud, normally this section of the route is a well-beaten trail and even late into the day there will be groups on the mountain making route-finding pretty obvious.

Get onto the rocks and climb the ridge more or less direct, making good use of the steel belay posts that mark the route, to the top of the Klein Glockner. Exposed with sustained scrambling of Grade II+.

The crossing of the Glockner Scharte is the crux of the route, meaning that if you have found the ascent to the Klein Glockner difficult you would be advised to stay put and be happy with your success thus far, remembering that you are still higher than other mountains in Austria except for the last few metres of the Gross Glockner itself.

During the season the area around the scharte needs to be treated with care as it can be a bit of a zoo as various groups vie for position and ropes, along with tempers and nerves, get crossed. The scharte itself is a knife-edged arête being no more than 5–6m across, with little protection for the leader or second until it is crossed.

Well worn rocks lead to the summit of Gross Glockner

Descend the 15m or so into the Glockner Scharte down a difficult step making use of the stout fixed ropes which aid the route: the rocks on the last few metres are undercut, adding to the challenge. Cross the *scharte* and exit on the other side. Now climb the steep ridge, grade II+, exposed, with steel belay posts in place, the remaining few metres to the summit with its large wooden cross (1½hrs).

THE VIEW FROM GROSS GLOCKNER

On a good day the view from the summit is one of the best in the Alps. To the south the whole of the Dolomites are stretched out with the white crown of the Marmolata, Queen of the Dolomites, being quite obvious. Nearer at hand to the west is the unmistakable snowy mantel of the Gross Venediger which retains the title of having the most connected glaciers in Austria. Sharp eyes that have spent time in the Venediger will be able to pick out the Drei Herrn Spitze and the snowy slopes of the Simony Spitze.

Further a field and not so obvious is the Zillertal's Grosser Loeffler and Schwarzenstein on the Italian border. Of adjacent peaks the aspects of the Grosses Wiesbachhorn and Johannisberg are particularly fine. Lastly various huts are easily picked out, starting with the Adlersruhe then around to the tourist complex Franz Josef Haus, Hofmanns Hut and lastly the Oberwalder make the whole scene complete and something to remember.

To descend, return by the same route to the Erzherzog Johann Hut (2hrs) or Studl Hut (4hrs). See also the next route description for an alternative descent route from the Adlersruhe to Glockner Haus via the Meletzkigrat ridge.

The thing to remember about the Gross Glockner is that while the mountain is highly accessible there are no easy routes on the mountain and while the normal route as described here is very straightforward it involves a glacier crossing and sustained scrambling with rock climbing sections of grade II+. Sections of the route also provide jaw-dropping exposure, particularly the upper section ▶

of the Klein Glockner and when negotiating the Glockner Scharte.

Thereafter the other main difficulty will come from aspirant alpinists on the mountain, with the added risk of ropes getting tangled, rocks being dislodged and folk just getting in the way of each other.

Needless to say since this is a very high mountain and as such the route needs to be undertaken in relatively good weather and when both the Gross and Klein Glockner are snow-free.

1.2 Erzherzog Johann Hut to Glockner Haus via the Meletzkigrat (alternative descent from Gross Glockner)

Standard time	6hrs
Ascent	200m but mostly descent (around 1500m)
Distance	11km

Should you have overnighted at the Erzherzog Johann Hut you will find this alpine day full of challenge and scenic variety and a very worthy alternative in seeing another aspect of the Glockner even if it is at the expense of visiting the Salm Hut.

Whether this route is undertaken after climbing the Gross Glockner only you can decide. However, despite its length this is very much an alpine day out that embraces everything one can expect from an alpine journey, from simple walking to glaciers to rock climbing and lots of challenge.

The initial part of the journey is best undertaken in twilight, to experience the dawn patrol and witness the sun illuminating the top of the Gross Glockner. You may have to wait for a while, until the sun clears the

Adlersruhe, for the shadows to disappear from the Meletzkigrat and the whole world to open up before proceeding.

Although hard in descent the Meletzkigrat is seen as a worthy alternative to descending through the Hofmanns Kees glacier direct, which is now very difficult, being steep and potentially dangerous in its middle section due to the onslaught of global warming. The Meletzki, on the other hand, offers challenging ground on warm rock, suitably protected with bolts when required to get around awkward ground, that takes in the very best of alpine scenery with time to ponder that not so long ago the level of the Pasterzen Kees glacier was almost up to the Hofmanns Hut and Franz Josef Haus. Despite this the Pasterzen Kees remains the longest glacier in Austria and the Eastern Alps.

On the last leg of the journey ambling down the Pasterzen Kees glacier, participants will be constantly looking back to the Gross Glockner as some of the satellite peaks come into clearer perspective, particularly the Johannisberg surrounded by a sea of glaciers. This is a long but exceptional promenade. Enjoy.

On the Meletzkigrat

From the hut climb the rocks immediately behind the hut to the upper reaches of the Hofmanns Kees glacier (15mins). Tackle up, get onto the glacier and make a descending traverse northeast to the head of an obvious ridge on the 3300m contour, the Glocknerkamp, better known in the climbing world as the Meletzkigrat (½hr).

Stow ice tools and sort climbing gear as the route now follows the ridge for the next 2hrs amid superb scenery overlooking the Hofmanns Kees and Pasterzen Kees glaciers.

Get onto the ridge and make a descending traverse east following the crest of the ridge or by turning various towers, pinnacles and obstacles on the right, south. The route is not always obvious and there are a number of places midway which appear to offer easier ground on the south flank. Avoid this temptation and look for evidence of climbers, as the most difficult bits, with moves of grade II+ have in situ bolts for protection or as abseil points. The ridge eventually relents at a point known as the Breakfast Stop (Fruehstucksplatz) at 2800m, equipped with a marker pole for climbers heading in the other direction (2hrs).

The main difficulties passed, the ridge eases a little with the route of sorts continuing east then north down steep rocks over difficult broken ground with the more serious sections equipped with fixed wires to gain the moraines of the Pasterzen Kees glacier (1hr).

The foot of the ridge is a jumbled mass of loose rocks and ice rubble with a vague trail marked by the odd stone cairn and splash of paint indicating the way to the glacier. Continue northeast, weaving in and out of the boulders making a direct line for the Hofmanns Hut which in good weather is clearly visible on the opposite bank, followed by a flattish ten minute walk until you are roughly in the middle of the glacier. Hereabouts head southeast down the Pasterzen Kees glacier to the signpost at the foot of the Franz Josef Haus tourist complex (1hr).

Continue south across the ice-sculptured rocky slopes of the Moell, heading down over the old moraines overlooking the watershed outflow of streams emerging from the Pasterzen Kees glacier, to a footbridge to get across the gorge above the Stausee Margaritzen reservoir. Follow this rocky trail through the aptly-named Stein Garden to its base, then circumnavigate around the south end of reservoir to the signpost at the dam wall (1hr).

Proceed along the dam wall, taking time to wonder where all the ice went from the glacier over the past 200 years, and then climb the track that follows the service road to eventually emerge at the Glockner Haus with all its finery, in total contrast to the Adlersruhe (30mins).

Alternatively, from the foot of Franz Josef Haus get the funicular railway for the five minute ride to the large car and coach parking area at Gletscherblick and the start of the *Promenadeweg* (tourist trail), which goes through various tunnels with audio-visual displays, emerging each time with brilliant views back across the void to the Gross Glockner and up the Pasterzen Kees glacier to the snow-encrusted Johannisberg. ▶

This is a good place for a break and something to eat at the restaurant.

From the tourist complex proceed down the road for 10mins then, just before the avalanche tunnels, bear right at the signpost and descend the steep slopes and rock cleft at Pointbalfen. Get across the footbridge and follow the path up the other side to the Pasterzen Haus, followed by a five minute stroll down the road to Glockner Haus (1hr).

The main difficulties with this route are threefold aside from the fact that it should only be undertaken in good, settled weather.

Firstly, it is quite a long way and that in itself demands that participants should be fit and used to carrying a touring rucksack for hours on end.

Secondly, it demands a reasonable skill level in as much that participants should be comfortable on all the types of ground that will be crossed including some not so pleasant.

Last, there is no escape route once you are committed to the route until the foot of the ridge when an effective way off the mountain can be made via the Franz Josef Haus tourist complex.

1.3 Ascent of the Romariswandkopf

Standard time	5hrs
Distance	4km
Ascent	740m

An exercise in glacier travel. This is an excellent glacier promenade full of scenic interest and challenge, that is unfortunately much neglected due to its close proximity to the Gross Glockner.

The first part of the route is dominated by views of the Studl Grat and the west face of the Gross Glockner, topped with its large crucifix and flanked by the jagged ridge of the Teufelkamp. Midway along the glacier the views open up across the void to the Gross Venediger with its extensive glacier system. It is, however, the crux of the route that will hold the attention for a while as the steep ground around the crevasse-cum-*bergschrund* is negotiated, which is glacier scenery at its best. Once over the obstacle travel becomes less demanding as the upper slopes of the Fruschnitz Kees glacier are crossed and the final pull up to the summit.

From the hut pick up the trail to the Studl Grat heading north up a series of zigzags, vague in places and more problematic if you set out before dawn, climbing steadily over the shaley southern slopes and buttress of the '*Schere*' to point a at 2987m on the edge of the Teischnitz Kees glacier and foot of the Luisengrat (a short 1hr).

Tackle up and get onto the glacier edge, hugging the western side of the Luisengrat and following climber's tracks heading for the Studl Grat. Excellent views of the Gross Glockner and Studlgrat, which are in profile.

At a point a little north of the Luisen Scharte (3175m) make a diagonal traverse left, northwest, negotiating several banks of easy crevasses on the 3200m contour. ◀ At a point midway, head north to the western edge of the Glocknerwand and an obvious steepening slope in the glacier and crux of the route. Head for this and the now very obvious crevasse-cum-*bergschrund* that splits the

From here there are stunning views of the jagged ridge of the Glocknerwand.

EXCURSIONS FROM THE STUDL HUT

The route as seen from the Grosser Muntanitz

slope. Climb the steepening slopes northeast and cross the snow bridge to gain the upper slopes of the Fruschnitz Kees glacier. Excellent glacier scenery, plus the Gross Venediger shows itself to the west (2hrs).

Get onto the upper slopes of the Fruschnitz Kees glacier and head north then northwest past the foot of the Teufelskamp ('Devil's Ridge') followed by a similar distance to the prominent col of the Romariswand Sattel 3426m. Thereafter climb the obvious snow arête with a final scramble up the steep loose shattered rocks to the summit (1hr).

THE VIEW FROM THE ROMARISWANDKOPF

The views from the summit are exceptional, particularly the unusual view to the Gross Glockner but the great glacier system to the north leading around to the Johanniberg (3463m), Hohe Riffl (3346m), then further afield the great bulk of the Grosses Weisbachhorn (3570m). Closer at hand across the Dorfertal valley are the peaks of the Granat Group, the Grosser Muntanitz, Granat Spitze and finally the Stubacher Sonnblich, while those with very sharp eyes will be able to locate the Rudolfs Hut/Berg Hotel at the edge of the Weissee.

Difficult ground on the Fruschnitz Kees glacier

Like all glacier journeys this route is subject to change from year to year, more so now with the effects of global warming. The crux of the route is in crossing the bank of crevasses on the 3380m contour to gain the upper snow slopes of the Fruschnitz Kees glacier. If there has been a good winter snow fall then most of the open crevasses will have been filled in, if not then crossing the big crevasse that splits the lower slope from the upper will be very problematic and you should enquire from the hut guardian before setting out.

An alternative route is to continue at a lower level on the 3300m contour, and make for the rocky ridge that splits the glacier above the Gramulsattel. This too is defended by a bank of crevasses, though not as serious as the upper slope there are a lot more of them.

This route is an exercise in glacier travel but it is not a route to contemplate in dodgy weather and is better early in season.

STAGE 2
Studl Hut to Salm Hut via the Pfort Scharte

Standard time 2½–3hrs
Distance 5km
Ascent About 300m
See map on page 136.

One of the finest promenades of the Rucksack Route though a little short on duration. This is a fine outing that follows in the footsteps of those early mountaineers who pioneered the first ascent and early routes on the Gross Glockner. The early part of the route is characterised by a descending traverse that contours around the slopes of the Keesbalfen and Langer Trog high above the Koednitztal valley. Unfortunately views of the Gross Glockner are lost until the material goods hoist is reached at Murztaler Steig, when the views of the mountain are restored, albeit for a short time. Thereafter the steep but short 250m+ of ascent up the Pfort Scharte is very much a bum up and brain out of gear affair that is only relieved on reaching the col when the Salm Hut comes into view.

Crossing the watershed at Nassfeld where many streams congregate views of the Gross Glockner are restored and once at the pleasant Salm Hut sharp eyes will be able to locate the Adlersruhe perched on the ridge high above.

From the hut proceed to the Fanat Scharte signpost and follow the signs and path for the Gross Glockner, where after a few minutes the path breaks right at another **signpost**. Proceed east on the Johann Studl Weg and gradually make a descending traverse following a good rocky trail over several bridges down into the glacial basin of Sandriegl. There is a signpost for the Gross Glockner and Adlersruhe and marked by the additional presence of the **seilbahn** (materials/goods hoist) pylons (a short 1hr).

Continue as before south but now on Route 713 where after a few minutes a **signpost** indicating the way to the Salm Hut and Luckner Haus is reached. Ascend more steeply following a line of fixed **wire ropes** to round the buttress of the Langer Trog that eventually leads after ½hr to a **signpost** at the foot of the Pfort Scharte.

Proceed northeast up the steep, shaley path, twisting and turning to and fro to the Pfort Scharte (2828m), from where the Salm Hut is clearly visible across the void to the east (¾hr).

From the col, descend steep difficult ground northeast for 100m over loose shale and scree until the ground gradually eases. Then down steep zigzags over rocks to the junction of paths coming from the Glorer Hut (½hr).

Cross the various streams of the Nassfeld watershed over marshy ground east, with good views of the Gross Glockner, followed by easy ground to the hut (½hr).

Looking toward Schwerteck from Pfort Scharte with the ruins of the first and second Salm Huts

THE FIRST AND SECOND SALM HUTS

While descending from the col take a few minutes to search the cliff face of Schwerteck on the opposite side of the valley, from where sharp eyes will be able to locate the remains of the second Salm Hut tucked tight into the rock face on the track to the Adlersruhe that, from a distance looks, like a pair of eyes staring out across the void. Further down the track, while negotiating the steep zigzags stop for a while and try to visualise the former extent of the Leiter Kees glacier that covered the whole area up to the height of the second Salm Hut and down to the moraines where the original Salm Hut was located. While scanning the scene try to pick out the ruins of the original Salm Hut located in the centre of the Nassfeld watershed and marked by cairns, where the pasture land merges with the boulders and general rubble of the once mighty Leiter Kees glacier.

STAGE 3
Salm Hut to Glockner Haus

Standard time   2½–3hrs
Distance   6km
Ascent   Around 250m
See map on page 136.

In terms of pure walking this promenade is probably the best walk of the entire Rucksack Route and Runde Tour: should you be blessed with good weather then alpine walking does not come much better than this. The first hour is almost effortless delightful walking traversing the slopes high above the Leitertal valley. Then comes a gentle reminder that you are in the mountains and cannot be complacent, as the path goes vertical to get round difficult ground at Lackner Ofen. Once this little difficulty is passed the Stocker Scharte is quickly reached and provides the promenade's 'wow' factor when the whole of the Pasterze valley opens up with a stunning view up the Pasterzen Kees glacier, topped at its head by the snowy mantle of the Johannisberg (3453m), named after Archduke Johann and flanked by the Hohe Riffl (3338m).

From the hut proceed east on a well-marked trail following Route 741 along the Wiener Hoehen Weg, traversing the slopes on the 2500m contour around the rocky flank of Schwerteck (3247m) high above the Leitertal valley. This is absolutely delightful walking with superb scenery. ◄

After about 20mins or so, take time to scan the hillside for the colonies of marmot that reside on the slopes aptly named Schwertboden.

The pleasant walking comes to an abrupt end after 1hr, when the trail picks up pace to negotiate the steep open slopes of Lackner Ofen which, once climbed via a natural cleft in the rock face, descends equally as dramatically on the other side, with **fixed wires**, leading ultimately to the panoramic viewpoint at Stocker Scharte (2501m) overlooking the whole of the Pasterzen Kees glacier, the tourist enclave of Franz Josef Haus and Stausee Margaritze (a short 1hr). Fabulous scenery hereabouts.

From the viewpoint, with the Glockner Haus clearly in view, descend steep difficult ground for 100m until the ground eases into a series of long looping zigzags, steep in places, until they come to a natural end at the stausee dam wall (¾hr).

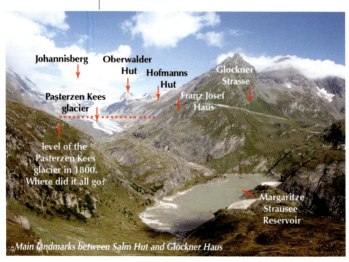

Main landmarks between Salm Hut and Glockner Haus

STAGE 3 – SALM HUT TO GLOCKNER HAUS

Johannisberg from Franz Josef Haus

THE VIEW FROM THE STOCKER SCHARTE

While the Pasterze still remains the longest single glacier in the eastern Alps its glory has long passed and from the vantage point of the Stocker Scharte it is clear to see from the moraines that line the glacier that it once covered the whole area up to the height Franz Josef Haus. Thereafter sharp eyes will then be needed to locate the Oberwalder Hut perched on its rocky knoll. Closer at hand above Franz Josef Haus is the Hofmanns Hut.

Proceed along the dam wall, taking time to wonder where all the ice went from the glacier over the past 200 years, then take the track that follows the service road to emerge eventually at the Glockner Haus with all its finery, in total contrast to the Salm Hut (½hr).

STAGE 4

Glockner Haus to Fusch via the Phandl Scharte

Standard time	6 to 7hr
Distance	12km to Ferleiten, 19km to Fusch
Ascent	550m

This is a fine promenade characterised by raw mountain scenery: while not rating high in terms of scenery this route rates very high as a mountain day. The initial part of the route is pleasant alpine walking with good retrospective views of the Gross Glockner. Unfortunately as height is gained those views are soon lost and replaced with rawer mountain scenery, snow and boulder-strewn slopes, evident around the former Sudlicher Pfandl Scharten Kees glacier just below the Pfandl Scharte.

Once across the col with its large crucifix that feeling of wilderness is further enhanced as more rock and ice is encountered and while such wilderness scenery is great to see you also get the feeling that this is not a place to get caught out, despite a fabulous view all the way down the Fuschertal valley. Once across the Pfandlbach stream it is an exceedingly long way down into the valley, descending 1100m in 4km, with endless zigzags down the Spaherbrunnl hillside that only end with the particularly pleasant walk through the meadows of Fuschertal to the small hamlet at Ferleiten, then the short distance to the main road, and Glocknerstrasse at Wild Park.

From Glockner Haus cross the Glocknerstrasse road to the signpost by the bus stop. Proceed northeast following Route 702/728 up steep but easy ground following the well-marked trail across the high alpine pasture land of **Troegeralm**.

Excellent retrospective views back toward the Gross Glockner. After 1hr or so, with the Pfandl Scharte clearly in view, the trail picks up pace as the ground becomes more enclosed and demanding, making a sudden turn to

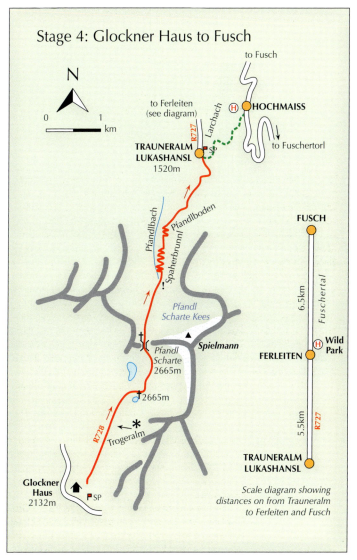

Windy conditions at the Pfandl Scharte 2663m

the right, east, descending over rocks and boulders to the glacial tarn at a point at 2665m. ◄

There is good wilderness-type scenery hereabouts, with the Pfandl Scharte clearly in view.

Rounding the tarn the path of sorts descends steep difficult ground over rocks and boulders into the glacial basin of what remains of the Sudlicher Pfandl Scharten Kees glacier. Cross through the basin over streams and glacial debris of rocks and boulders, keeping an eye open for the route markers as they interweave through the glacial debris heading north to the Untere Phandl Scharte (2663m) with its broad saddle and large **crucifix**, complete with record book, marking the ancient trade route between valleys (2hrs). ◄

Enjoy the excellent view from here down the Fuschertal valley toward Ferleiten and Fusch.

From here onwards the next 1½hrs of the descent down the valley can be split into three distinct sections, the first two demanding a reasonable amount of mountaineering skill. From the col proceed north down the snow slope of what remains of the Nordlicher Pfandl Scharten Kees glacier. If you have crampons with you, you are advised to tackle up and wear them, if not proceed with care down the snow until it is possible to gain the left hand edge of the snow and lateral moraine west; look for marker posts. Proceed down the snow or moraines that are loose and grotty until the ground eases on the 2300m contour (½hr).

Thereafter, continue as before descending over difficult ground of loose rocks, boulders and shale that gradually steepens and forces you to the head of the Pfandlbach glacial stream that has to be crossed. Descend to the stream's edge over loose rocks; choose your spot carefully as there are few places to cross and all are precarious (½hr).

Pick up the trail on the east side of the stream that soon leads to a monotonous series of zigzags descending the **Pfandlboden** overlooking the Fuschertal valley until they come to a natural end at the farms at Lukashansl and Trauneralm the signpost at the junction of the path leading to the car park on the Glocknerstrasse at Hochmaiss (½hr).

At the group of farm buildings the signpost states that it is 1hr to Ferleiten and 2½hrs to Fusch. Have none of this and be content with reaching the hamlet of Ferleiten and the Glocknerstrasse toll gate within 2hrs.

From Trauneralm follow the single track graded road down through the forest and woodland of spruce and larch aptly named Larchach, now on Route 727, twisting and turning until the trail reaches the valley floor from where effortless walking leads through high alpine meadows following the Fuscher Ache river for 4km to the Glocknerstrasse main road at Wild Park and a complex of tourist-orientated buildings (a short 2hrs).

From Wild Park you have the choice of walking all the way to Fusch: this will take a further 2hrs. Alternatively you can wait for the local bus service to Fusch or you can go into the information centre and order a taxi from Fusch to come and collect you.

For accommodation in Fusch you can make enquiries at the Tourist Information Office at Wild Park or alternatively the author can recommend the Gasthof Wasserfall is close by the path leading to the Gleiwitzer Hut for Stage 5 of the route.

Up to the point of crossing the Pfandl Scharte the route is quite straightforward, whereas once the pass is crossed caution and mountain awareness need to be exercised. Descending the Nordlicher Pfandl Scharten Kees glacier which is very straightforward if you have crampons, requiring no more skill than a walk down steepish snow for 20mins. If on the other hand you don't have crampons then you have two options: firstly, try the snow and hope you don't slither about too much; or, alternatively, opt for the very loose ground at the edge of the snow and hope the ground doesn't slide with you.

Having gained relative security off the snow slope, the next challenge will be to cross the Pfandlbach. While the Pfandlbach is a stream, it is a glacial stream of serious proportions and being glacial it is full of boulders. Following the track you are led into a dead end as the track peters out, gradually forcing you down to the stream's edge. As you approach the stream look for the red path marker painted on a largish boulder on the opposite bank, then choose your crossing point carefully and make good use of your trekking poles to aid stability. Hopefully as the Glockner Round becomes more popular the National Park Authority will commission a bridge to be built.

Finally, this is not a route to undertake in poor weather, as the difficulties of navigating through the boulders around the Sudlicher Pfandl Scharten Kees, then descending the Nordlicher Pfandl Scharten Kees's snow slopes, and finding the correct place to cross the Pfandlbach stream, would be very problematic. It would be safer and wiser to declare a rest day and take the local bus to Fusch.

STAGE 5
Fusch to Gleiwitzer Hut

Standard time	4hrs
Distance	5km, 6km if you count the zigzags
Ascent	1360m

See overview map on page 130.

A pleasant outing with a substantial amount of uphill mostly in the forest.

If you stayed at the Landgasthof Wasserfall, as recommended, then from the *gasthof* turn left and walk down the road for a short distance and turn left again, where you will find a signpost for the Gleiwitzer Hut. Alternatively from the village church follow signs for the Gleiwitzer Hut through pretty chalet type houses heading west and eventually picking up Route 725 at the foot of the forest.

Approaching Hirzbach Alm with the Gleiwitzer Hut clearly visible

Follow the forest track through Feistalpl for 2hrs, zig-zagging through pleasant forest scenery, steep in places, until a substantial footbridge across the Hirzbach river is reached. Continue as before heading west as the forest gradually clears to reveal the Gleiwitzer Hut perched on the rocky knoll of the Edelweisskopferl, named, no doubt, on account of the Edelweiss flowers that can be found on its slopes. After a kilometre or so the farm of Hirzbach Alm (1715m) is reached, at a signpost (2½hrs).

The trail now curves west to the left then, as the signpost states, it is 1¼hrs to the hut, climbing steadily up the slopes of Edelweisskopferl through high alpine pasture and scrub alpine rose bushes via the usual series of zigzags to the very pleasant Gleiwitzer Hut.

Excellent views back down the valley toward Fusch then across the void to the Dachstein Mountains in the north and the Tennen Gebirge, Austria's Dolomite range, on the eastern horizon.

STAGE 6
Gleiwitzer Hut to Heinrich Schwaiger Haus

Standard time	8–10hrs
Distance	8km
Ascent	A lot of up and down but about 1650m

The premiere day of the Rucksack Route full of scenic interest and challenge and not for the faint hearted. This is without doubt the best promenade of the whole Glockner Rucksack Route and while not strictly on the Glockner Runde Tour its inclusion as a mountain day beats anything else the Rucksack Route has to offer, even if the purpose of visiting the Heinrich Schwaiger Haus is really to climb the Grosses Weisbachhorn. The challenges of the route start very early on as the trail leads to a dead end equipped with metal pegs and staples used to gain the tiny col and ridge at the Untere ▶

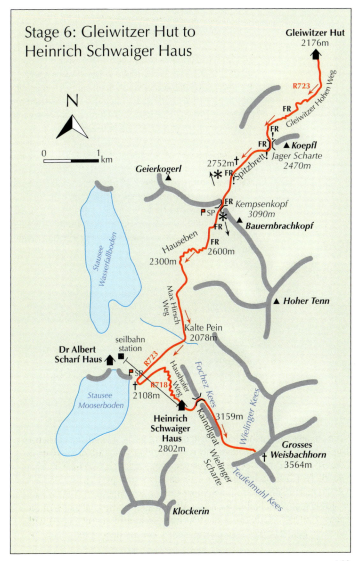

Jager Scharte. Thereafter climbing the Spitzbrett ridge is superb scrambling territory, very exposed but well-protected by wire ropes and handrails that run the entire length of the ridge from the Untere Jager Scharte at 2470m to the Kempsenkopf at 3090m. 600m of pure mountain pleasure. Once over the main col at Kempsenkopf the mountain scenery opens up and is truly superb, particularly across the void to the big glaciated peaks of the Grosses Weisbachhorn and Hohe Riffl, complemented by the Stausee Mooserboden reservoir down in the valley. If you have the weather with you this is a very good day in the mountains. Enjoy.

Be on your way early, and no later than 07:00hrs: while various signs say 8hrs, allow all day as 10hrs is not uncommon.

From the hut proceed south along Route 723 along a well marked path of upper alpine pasture below the slopes of the Vorderes Spitzbrett and Krapfbrachkopf along the Gleiwitzer Hohen Weg heading for an enclosed cirque that eventually leads over rocks with **fixed ropes** to a dead end below the Koepfl 2518m (1hr).

If you have climbing equipment with you, tackle up with a rudimentary harness, sling and karabiner, then proceed to climb a row of staples and steel pegs up a rock cleft to reach the ridge of the Untere Jager Scharte (2470m) (1hr).

From hereon, proceed southwest along the Spitzbrett ridge, that is steep and very exposed making good use of the **fixed ropes** and handrails until the ridge comes to a natural end at the Obere Jagerschartl (2752m) (1hr).

The route turns now south to follow the steep ridge following a handrail of **fixed wire ropes**, very exposed in places, over difficult ground, until that also comes to a natural end at the Kempsenkopf col (3090m), the high point of the route (1hr). There are great views from here back down the Spitzbrett ridge and Hirzbachtal valley and across the void to the large lake at Zell am See and the mountains of the Dachstein.

From the col, proceed as before southwest and descent 400m down very steep difficult ground following

STAGE 6 – GLEIWITZER HUT TO HEINRICH SCHWAIGER HAUS

Approaching the Untere Jager Scharte with climbers on the Spitzbrett ridge

A Gr Weisbachhorn
B Kaindl Grat
C Heinrich Schwaiger Haus
D Johannisberg
E Hohe Riffl
F Mooserboden Stausee

Fabulous views from the Kempsen Kopf

a natural fault line and cleft protected by **fixed wires** (1½hrs). Fabulous views across the void from where sharp eyes will be able to locate Heinrich Schwaiger Haus, the more obvious Grosses Weisbachhorn (3564m) and the Stausee Mooserboden reservoir.

Thereafter the ground eases and turns west down a series of zigzags over grassy ground to a large red and white marker post at Hauseben on the 2300m contour (1½hrs). Round the hillside and proceed south on the Max Hirsch Weg following a grassy trail, vague in places until a congregation of streams is reached at Kalte Pein (2078m) (½hr). ◄

This is good place to take a break with good water.

While descending take time to check out the route along the edge of the reservoir to the Kapruner Torl and route to the Rudolfs Hut.

From here proceed southwest, following a rocky trail that eventually leads to a graded track associated with construction work for the reservoir and **signpost** at a junction of paths to the Heinrich Schwaiger Haus, slightly above the Stausee Mooserboden dam wall (1hr).

STAGE 6 – GLEIWITZER HUT TO HEINRICH SCHWAIGER HAUS

From here you have the option of continuing the journey unaided or make a short hour's detour by descending to the reservoir and crossing the dam wall to make use of the hut's material/goods hoist (*seilbahn*) and have your rucksack delivered to the hut.

Whatever your choice, from the junction of paths proceed southeast up the steep rocky trail that is the Haushofer Weg, aided by fixed wires and rope handrails following the obligatory zigzags for the 700m of ascent to the hut (2hrs). Just below the hut when you are feeling all but done in, there is an encouraging sign that says 'HSH 5 minutes'. Excellent views across the Stausee Mooserboden.

Escape Route

Should you be unfortunate enough to experience bad weather while at the Gleiwitzer Hut, preventing you doing this particular stage, take the track on Route 723 across the Brandl Scharte and descend to the car park for the Gletscherbahn bus service to and from Kaprun. From the car park Postbus 660 will take you as far as Kesselfall Alpenhaus. This is followed by an innovative open-top funicular-type transport arrangement that will deliver you at the Mooserboden reservoir dam wall, from where you can make the journey to the Heinrich Schwaiger Haus or, if you have overnighted elsewhere, proceed along the reservoir to pick up the route to the Rudolfs Hut.

The main consideration with this route is that it is a long way and quite demanding. The initial part of the journey is straightforward; however, once you reach the base of the Untere Jager Scharte the whole character of the route changes from alpine walking to scrambling 900m uphill followed by 400m downhill, taking around 5hrs. The climb throughout is very steep and although the route is protected by fixed wires the ground dropping away from the ridge is very exposed indeed, which means a slip or ▶

a trip would be very hard to stop and the resulting tumble down the mountainside would have serious consequences, hence my advice to equip yourself with a rudimentary harness of sling and karabiner to clip into the fixed wires. See Alpine Walking Skills in the Introduction.

Because of the demands of the route it goes without saying that it should be only undertaken in reasonably settled weather as it is no place to be caught in a thunderstorm and not a place to practise navigation and other mountain skills.

Should you be physically done in by the time you reach the Mooserboden reservoir and are too exhausted to contemplate the 700m climb to the hut, overnight accommodation is available at Fuerthermoaralm, but you would need to check beforehand if there are vacancies (tel 0043 (0) 6547 1582 3435).

This is a big day out set in high alpine territory: be on your way early.

EXCURSION FROM HEINRICH SCHWAIGER HAUS

6.1 Ascent of the Grosses Weisbachhorn

Standard time	4hrs
Distance	1km+
Ascent	760m

The Weisbachhorn is a big mountain in every sense of the word and one of the premiere peaks of the Glockner Group. A justifiably popular route up

Excursions from Heinrich Schwaiger Haus

one of the Glockner Groups biggest mountains as the Weisbachhorn is huge and overlooks everything in the area, being particularly fine when seen from the Gross Glockner.

Once on the summit, if you are blessed with good weather the Gross Glockner shows itself, towering over all the neighbouring peaks. Further afield to the west are the Granat Spitze and Stubacher Sonnblick, then behind those peaks is the Gross Venediger.

From the back of the hut, follow signs for the mountain heading east. After a few minutes of steady climbing the route reaches a set of fixed wires to climb through a near vertical steep cleft for 100m or so. Climb this, then follow route markers over steep ground zigzagging to and fro to reach a small col at the Interer Fochezkopf (3022m) after a short hour.

From the col, proceed southeast up the prominent ridge over looking what remains of the Fochez Kees glacier to the Oberer Fochezkopf at a point at 3159m. Continue as before south along the splendid Kaindlgrat

On the Kaindlgrat with the Heinrich Schwaiger Haus green roof to the left

ridge with excellent mountain scenery toward the Wiesbachhorn west face with the summit cross in view. Keep to the west side of the ridge to avoid unnecessary exposure at the edge of the Wielinger Kees glacier, following the ridge to its natural end at the junction of the Teufelmuhel Kees glacier (½hr).

THE KAINDLGRAT

The Kaindlgrat is named after Alfred Kaindl, who was a pioneer of routes on the mountain and who helped finance and build the original Heinrich Schwaiger Haus in 1872, prior to the hut being known by that name. The snow arête has all but disappeared over the years apart from the section on the approach to the foot of the west ridge. While on the ridge spend some time to remember that Herr Kaindl would have made the climb direct from the valley without the aid of public transport. Also note that the famous German alpinist Wilo Welzenbach would have made the same approach across these slopes en route to his first ascent of the northwest face in 1924, a route that has now largely disappeared apart from winter ascents.

Tackle up and cross the short section of exposed snow arête for 200m to gain the foot of the west ridge (½hr). From here follow the ridge east over rocks and boulders, some of dubious quality, to the summit cross. Extensive views in all directions (1hr).

In descent either retrace your steps back down the west ridge or make the decent via the southwest ridge and west flank to the foot of the Wielinger Scharte, then head north to pick up the Kaindlgrat ridge and back to the hut.

The rock quality on the west ridge of the Wiesbachhorn is very poor and demands to be treated with caution. In descent the neighbouring southwest ridge is marginally better with less exposure.

The only other hazard is that the route can be very windy and this can pose very real risks of being blown over by gusts as the author can testify, needless to say that the mountain should only be climbed in reasonably settled weather.

STAGE 6A
Gleiwitzer Hut to Kaprun via the Brandl Scharte

Standard time	3½–4hrs
Distance	5km
Ascent	200m

The official Glockner Runde Tour actually ends at the Gleiwitzer Hut and descends to Kaprun, while this guidebook's Glockner Rucksack Route continues to the Heinrich Schwaiger Haus. Should you wish to end the tour here then the following brief route description is offered.

From the signpost at the hut proceed north along a good track on Route 723. After 10mins a signpost is reached indicating the way to the Brandl Scharte. Take the left-hand branch and follow the zigzags up the hillside to the Brandl Scharte (1hr). From the col proceed northwest down to the Rosskopf and Harleitenalm to eventually emerge at the Kaprun Glacier Railway car park and local bus service to Kaprun (2½hrs).

STAGE 7

Heinrich Schwaiger Haus to Rudolfs Hut/Berg Hotel via Kapruner Torl

Standard time	7–8hrs
Distance	9km
Ascent	860m

A pleasant outing through some interesting scenery but something of an anti-climax compared to the previous day's outing, but still there are a number of places along this stage worthy of mention. The first is the actual Kapruner Torl, or gate, a tiny notch in the ridge through which you have to pass. The second is at the end of the path above the debris-strewn Tor Kees glacier from where just before the zigzags descend; it is possible to see boulders with splashes of paint and route markers that indicate the original path that was obliterated by a huge rock fall from the cliffs above the slopes of the Ubelkar. It is around here that the best scenery of the day can be seen, with excellent views across the void to the Granat Spitze and Stubacher Sonnblick. Thirdly, once down in the glacial basin passing through the chaos of house sized boulders is quite amazing, and it is reassuring to think that you were not around when they came tumbling down off the mountain. Finally, by the time you reach the choice of paths over or around the Schafbichl (a small peak where sheep graze) take the left hand fork on the Steinere Steig as it is more enjoyable.

From the hut, take the path downhill to the Stausee Mooserboden dam wall (1¼hrs).

From the pump house pick up Route 716 and follow this southwest above the edge of the reservoir on a pleasant easy path until it comes to a **signpost** at a natural end (1hr).

Cross the **footbridge** and proceed over easy ground up a rocky path that is partially overgrown in places. Gradually the route picks up pace and starts to climb steadily following glacial moraines overlooking a small alpine tarn and the dead glacial moraines at Wintergasse.

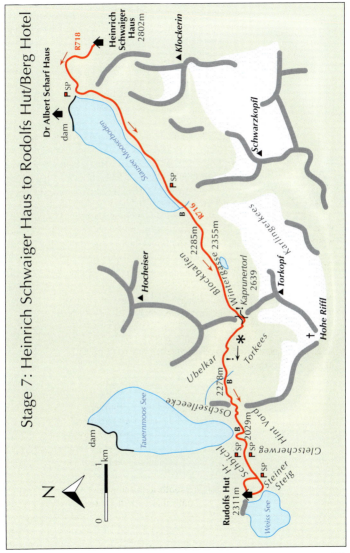

Thereafter cross over difficult ground with loose boulders, slabs and blocks and other ankle breaking terrain to arrive eventually at the tight little col that is the Kapruner Torl gate (2hrs).

From the col, proceed down over steep rocky ground to pick up the trail that traverses across the slopes of the Umbelkar northwest above what remains of the Tor Kees glacier. After about ½hr, at around the 2500m contour, sharp eyes will see a little of the Weissee reservoir and outbuildings of the Rudolfs Hut's cable car system to the west along with the peaks of the Stubacher Sonnblick and Granat Spitze. The Rudolfs Hut is hidden from view behind the little Hinterer Schafbichl peak. Continue as before but now on the edge of a lateral moraine that at its end descends steeply into a jumbled mass of house sized boulders. Proceed with some difficulty through the boulders until they peter out at a patch of marshy ground where a number of streams congregate at 2278m (1hr). Good place for a break.

Cross the footbridge and follow the path down the rocky slopes and cliffs between the Hintere and Vordere Oschsefleecke to a **footbridge** and **signpost** at the Tauern Moossee reservoir (1hr).

Robert Hampson negotiating house-sized boulders below the Tor Kees glacier

Follow the trail uphill overt marshy ground with scrub alpine rose bushes southwest, to a **signpost** at the junction of a path heading off to the Gletscherweg up the Odenwinkel Kees valley. After a short distance a second **signpost** is reached. The right fork declares the hut to be 45mins away via relatively easy ground that ascends the little peak of Hinterer Schafbichl, while the left fork declares the hut to be 40mins away via the Steinere Steig, rounding the rocky flank of the Schafbichl via a series of fixed wires and a short section of ladder that provides some good scenery toward the Hohe Riffl (1½hrs).

This promenade is quite straightforward with little in the way to hinder your progress. However the slopes just below the Kapruner Torl are boulder-strewn, with loose slabs and blocks that demand care. Similarly do not dwell at the house-sized boulders at the foot of the Tor Kees glacier as the area is still prone to rockfall. Both these places will be more problematic when snow-covered or if you are unfortunate enough to make this crossing in poor weather.

EXCURSIONS FROM RUDOLFS HUT

7.1 Ascent of the Stubacher Sonnblick and Granat Spitze

Standard time	4hrs
Ascent	830m
Distance	4km

As mountains just over the magical 3000m contour these two pose a real challenge. While the name 'Granat Spitze' appears to make reference to granite it is actually a reference to the mineral garnet.

If you are on your way early you should have sufficient time to make the crossing of the Kalser Tauern for an evening meal at the Kalser Tauern Haus or Sudetendeutsche Hut.

This is a very good promenade with some interesting scenery. At Seewande take time to study the glacial pond that has developed at the foot of the glacier over the past few years as a result of global warming. The pond and ice formations immediatly above are now subject of study by various institutions and glaciologists. In ascent of the Sonnblick Kees glacier there is little to see as the convex slope is always rising in front of you until you reach the Granat Scharte, where the route opens out to reveal the Venediger mountains to the west and the Glockner to the southeast, while those who climbed the Grosses Weisbachhorn will note its dominance to the east.

In terms of mountaineering, the Granat Spitze provides the better climbing as the rock is sounder than the Sonnblich. Accordingly if you have only time for one peak or are unsure about climbing both in the day then opt for the Granat Spitze as you can always bag the Sonnblich on the descent if you change your mind.

If you are on your way early, before the hut wakes up for breakfast, you can be up and down the mountain(s) and back at the hut for lunch, and by making use of the chair lift you can be at the Kalser Tauern just after midday, with plenty of time to get you to the Kalser Tauern Haus or the Sudetendeutsche Hut before dark. If you do that, then you really have had a good mountain day.

From the hut proceed north through the hut complex and down onto the dam wall of the man-made Weissee reservoir. It is well worth doing a recce of this beforehand as sometimes the doors around the basement level of the hut/hotel are locked, making life frustrating.

Cross the dam wall, which is used for ice-climbing in winter, to the far side, turning west, and climb up through a series of rock buttresses aided by a couple of short **ladders**, then zigzag through a rocky trail of sorts over blocks and boulders and other glacial debris leading into more open ground to a signpost at the glacial combe above the Seewande, overlooking the Sonnblick Kees glacier with its green icy pond (1hr).

Excursions from Rudolfs Hut

The Granat Group as seen from above the Odenwinkel Kees glacier

The route turns northwest, up a vague ridge over loose rocky ground, with good scenery across the glacier to the west and bounded by the cliffs on the right, until you are forced into a couloir-type basin then up steep zigzags and streams for a short distance to the foot of the glacier (½hr).

Tackle up and get onto the **Sonnblick Kees glacier** heading west up through the heart of the glacier towards the Sonnblick Scharte (2806m). Minimal crevasse danger. At a point around the 2760m contour turn southwest and start to climb up through the steepening glacier slopes hugging the rocks of the Sonnblick's northeast ridge and avoiding the steeper slopes and crevasses to the southeast until the glacier begins to level out around the 2900m contour (1hr). ▶

From here the summit cross of the Sonnblick is clearly visible as is the rocky pyramid of the Granat Spitze just short of a kilometre away.

Continue the final pull up on the glacier the short distance onto the **Granat Scharte** (2970m) where ice tackle may be dumped to make the final 100m scramble over blocks and slabs to the summit with its metal **cross** (½hr).

Trekking in Austria's Hohe Tauern

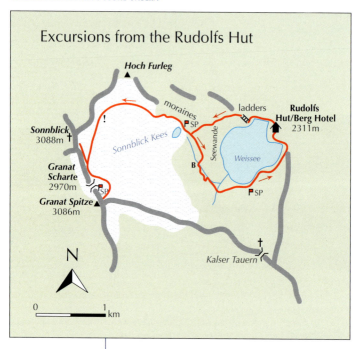

There are beautiful views of the Granat Spitze from here.

◂ From the Sonnblick summit, return to the Granat Scharte and head south easterly across the head of the glacier to a point east of the summit and obvious small notch in the ridge (½hr).

Stow ice tools and climb the northeast ridge more or less directly, exposed in places, with short sections of grade II, good belays with fixed slings, to the summit (½hr). Excellent views particularly the of the Johannisberg.

In descent retrace your steps to the foot of the glacier, avoiding the temptation to cut the corner off the upper slopes that will lead you over steep convex slopes into a bank of big crevasses.

From the foot of the glacier retrace your steps to the col and junction of paths at a point at 2500m, from where

EXCURSIONS FROM RUDOLFS HUT

On the Granat Spitze summit

you have a choice of either returning to the Rudolfs Hut the same way or turning south and making an alternative descent following the Gletscher Panoramaweg along the southern edge of the Weissee.

> The only point at which caution needs to be exercised is in descending the glacier from the Granat Spitze and the temptation to cut the corner from the Granat Scharte. Because the slope is convex, it is always dropping away from you and you cannot see the crevasses until you are on them: they will then cost you time to negotiate. The other point to remember is that because the glacier is slipping down the hill at an increased rate, crevasses are going to open up as the Sonnblick Kees glacier gradually dies.

7.2 Gletscher Panoramweg – Round of the Weissee

Standard time	3hrs
Ascent	200m
Distance	4km

When the Rudolfs Hut was the National Mountain Centre one of its aims was to encourage people into the mountains. This tour was designed to provide day visitors with a full mountain day, experiencing a variety of terrain including a close encounter with a glacier. The route maybe undertaken in either direction, with anti-clockwise being described here.

From the hut proceed through the hut complex north and down onto the dam wall of the Weissee man-made reservoir. Cross the dam wall to the far side, turning west to climb up through a series of rock buttresses aided by a couple of short ladders, then zigzag through blocks and boulders and other glacial debris into more open ground and a large marker post and weather station overlooking the Sonnblick Kees glacier above the Seewande at 2500m (1½hrs).

From here the route continues as for climbing the Sonnblick and Granat Spitze and may be followed for a further 1hr or so for those wanting a better view of the glacier. Thereafter the terrain is strictly that of the mountaineer equipped with rope, ice axe and crampons.

From the Seewande the route turns south to descend via the southern shore of the Weissee along a well-marked trail over rocks and paved paths back to the hut.

STAGE 8

*Rudolfs Hut to Sudetendeutsche Hut
via the Gradetz Sattel*

Standard time	7–8hrs
Ascent	A lot of up and down, about 1050m
Distance	About 11km

This is a fine route, full of interest and one of the best long distance promenades of the whole tour, including crossing the highest pass on the tour: alpine walking at its very best with just a few challenges thrown in to make the promenade very special.

The day starts out with excellent scenery around the Weissee and local peaks Granat Spitze and Stubacher Sonnblick dominating the scene, peaks that will be more important to you if you climbed them from the Rudolfs Hut. Once across the Kalser Tauern pass the views open up with a splendid panorama down the Dorfertal valley. However once you are committed to the Silesia Hohenweg and well on the way to the Sudetendeutsche Hut it will be the Eiskogele that first grabs your attention, then suddenly just the tip of the Gross Glockner comes into view. By the time you have reached the high alpine pasture at In der Multer the Gross Glockner will show itself to be what it is and totally dominates the panorama to the east, with the Eisekogele and Romariswandkopf seeming a little insignificant. Sadly once across the Gradetz sattel and the Gross Glockner is consigned to memory.

In the information published by the National Park Authority and the Austrian Alpine Club, the Sudetendeutsche Hut forms part of the 'official' Glockner *Runde Tour*. Aside from its being a splendid hut, the main reason for its inclusion in this guidebook in preference to the Kalser Tauern Haus is that affords the opportunity to climb the Grosser Muntanitz (3232m) as a separate excursion.

Before the advent of the Rudolfs Hut and the clatter of cable cars and chair lift this particular crossing was an ancient trade route linking the Pinzgau valley and towns of Mittersill, Uttendorf, Kaprun and Zell in the north with Kals, Matrei and the Virgental valley in the south.

TREKKING IN AUSTRIA'S HOHE TAUERN

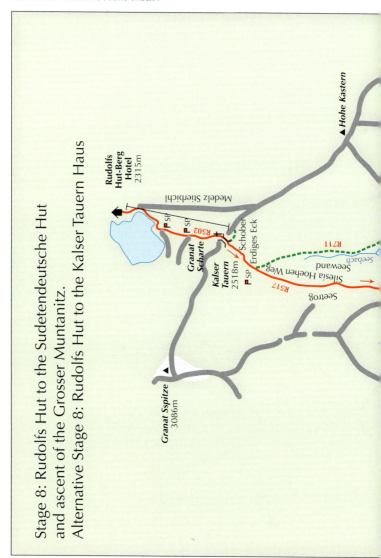

Stage 8: Rudolfs Hut to the Sudetendeutsche Hut and ascent of the Grosser Muntanitz.
Alternative Stage 8: Rudolfs Hut to the Kalser Tauern Haus

Stage 8 – Rudolfs Hut to Sudetendeutsche Hut

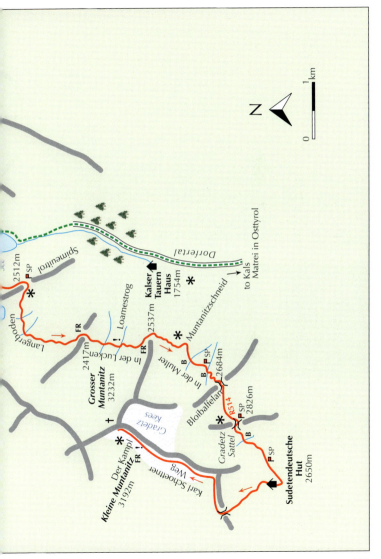

Leaving the pleasures of the Rudolfs Hut behind, proceed south across the dam wall of the man-made Weissee reservoir for 10mins to various signposts.

At the end of the dam turn left then right following signs for Kalser Tauern on Route 502, southwest, above the edge of the lake for around 10mins to a **signpost** at a junction of paths.

Now head south on Route 711, up the well-marked rocky trail running parallel with the Stierbichl Medelz rock buttress and chairlift, passing a large cairn about midway, at 2377m, which marked the previous route going off to the right on the St Poltener Way to the Granat Scharte and Karl Fuerst and Grunsee Huts. Continue as before south over rocky ground and onto the **Kalser Tauern pass** 2518m with its large crucifix and *torl* (gate) overlooking the Dorfertal and Stubachtal valleys (1hr).

Alternatively from the Rudolfs Hut, proceed south to the chairlift station and take a leisurely 10mins ride

At the Kalser Tauern pass 2513m

up the hogsback ridge of the Medelz buttress to the top station marked by many stone cairns, then ¼hr downhill to the Kalser Tauern. This is a good poor weather alternative. ▸

From the pass continue southwest, zigzagging down the slopes of the Schoeber along the well-marked trail, steep at first and frequently snow covered early in season, to the **signpost** at the junction of paths **Erdiges Eck** (2213m) and Route 711 heading south to the Kalser Tauern Haus.

Continue as before but now heading south along the Silesia Hohenweg and Route 517 progressing across the relatively easy ground of **Seetrog** that overlook the slopes of See Wand, climbing steadily over the broad terrace to an obvious saddle in the **Spinnevitrol** ridge at 2512m and junction of paths to the Kalser Tauern Haus (1hr). ▸

From the saddle proceed west then north to contour around the **Langerboden** open combe crossing several streams, followed by a steep pull up exposed rocks with **fixed wires** to a small col at point 2417m on the Luckenwand ridge (1hr). From here you can see the roof of the Kalser Tauern Haus.

From the ridge continue south over more difficult broken ground, crossing the first of several streams coming down from the high slopes of In der Lucken, culminating with a major glacial stream crossing that demands care and concentration to get across the Loamesbach. The way across the stream is waymarked but good alternatives also exist a little higher up. Choose your spot carefully and make good use of those trekking poles. Get over the stream and continue up the slopes of Loamestrog, climbing rocks with fixed ropes to a saddle at point 2537m (1hr).

Continue as before south, contouring around the high alpine hillside of **In der Multer**, frequently populated in summer by sheep and goats, to a broad saddle on the Muntanitzschneid ridge. Follow this around the hillside to join the track coming up from the Kalser Tauern Haus on Route 514, where our present Route 517 ends (1hr). ▸

There is excellent scenery on both sides of the Tauern pass.

There are good views down the Dorfertal valley to the Dorfer See and across the void to peaks of Eiskogele and the Romariswandkopf.

This is a good place for a break with excellent views toward the Gross Glockner and Romariswandkopf.

The route now turns southwest and picks up pace, zigzagging over steep rocky ground, crossing a couple of glacial streams in quick succession equipped with **bridges** to a subsidiary ridge at 2684m from where the Gradetz Sattel is visible. The trail now enters **Bloibalfelan**, a very barren place of pure rock with little vegetation that climbs steadily to the flat top of the Gradetz Sattel (2826m) with a **signpost** and a large stone cairn marking the highest pass on the Glockner Rucksack Route and *Runde Tour* (1hr).

Here, there are yet more fantastic views to the north of the Grosser Muntanitz and the last views of the tour toward the Gross Glockner.

◂ From the saddle, descend steep zigzags over difficult rocky ground that enters a flat glacial basin left behind by the retreating glacier. Cross the main glacial stream coming off Gradetz Kees glacier by a single plank wooden **bridge** and pick up a vague trail that descends by meandering through boulders and across patches of shaley ground, look for stone cairns and marker poles to a **signpost** at the junction of Route 502B heading to Kals via the Durrenfeld Scharte, the Sudetendeutsche Hut is now visible from here onwards just a few minutes away (1hr).

Despite the length and duration of this promenade there is very little to hinder your progress and no obstacles that have not been encountered before on the Rucksack Route. However the one place that is hazardous is the crossing of the glacial stream at Loamesbach. Hopefully a bridge will be constructed in the not too distant future. In the meantime proceed with caution.

Finally, due to the duration and length of the route this is not a journey to undertake in poor weather or on a falling barometer as there are few escape routes beyond the Kalser Tauern pass. The best option in poor weather conditions is to descend with relative ease and end the tour at the superb Kalser Tauern Haus.

EXCURSION FROM SUDETENDEUTSCHE HUT

8.1 Ascent of Grosser Muntanitz

Standard time   2½–3hrs
Ascent   600m
Distance   3km
See map on page 182.

The Muntanitz is a fine mountain that should be within the capabilities of most participants and is a fitting climb to end the Glockner Rucksack Route and *Runde Tour*. Once on the ridge the going is relatively easy though exposed, particularly on the 3110m contour that overlooks the rapidly diminishing Gradetz Kees glacier. The climb down the vertical cleft off the Kleiner Muntanitz provides the only climbing challenge of the route, being akin to climbing down the edge of a ship's prow.

From the hut, signpost, the route makes its way to the obvious Wellachkopf ridge on the skyline to the left, by first progressing up the rocky slopes, north, that top a small ridge to enter a glacial bowl of shale and sand yes sand, to make a rising diagonal reverse north to an obvious col at the western most point of the Wellachkopf ridge (¾hr).

Once on the ridge, either follow it east, by the track slightly below the crest, or with care tiptoe along the crest to a second col on the magic 3000m contour. The route now progresses below the ridge. Those who are vertigo-free may continue to follow the ridge, be careful if you do as there is exposed scrambling around the 3200m contour and visual evidence that the perma frost is slowly disappearing, leaving shear cracks at the edge of the ridge.

Continue to follow the ridge on the Karl Schoettner Weg to the foot of the Kleiner Muntanitz 3192m. Then

Ged O'Neill leading the start of the ridge on the ascent of the Grosser Muntanitz

descend a wide cleft in the near vertical rock face for twenty metres, very exposed, fixed wires in place, taking care at its foot to negotiate loose rocks until back on safer ground. Thereafter pick up the obvious trail once more and follow this to the broad saddle of der Kampl that marks the route coming up from the Gradetz Kees glacier, a route that has now almost all but disappeared into history due to the retreating ice, then over rocks and slabs to the summit with its large cross and fabulous views.

GROSSER MUNTANITZ

Grosser Muntanizt was first climbed on 2 September 1871 by Arthur von Schmit and his *bergfuehrer* friend Thomas Groder. The views from the summit are excellent, particularly towards the Romariswandkopf and Gross Glockner, with the Glockner dominating the scene to the east. Similarly, dominating the scene in the west is the Gross Venediger, then closer at hand to the north are the main peaks of the Granat Group, the Stubacher Sonnblich and the Granat Spitze. Finally for those with very sharp eyes the roof of the Kalser Tauern Haus can just be seen in the Dorfertal valley far below.

While the route is quite straightforward walking along the ridge, it is in places very exposed particularly the climb down off the Kleiner Muntanitz. A fall from here would have serious consequences. If you have your rudimentary harness with sling and karabiner it would be good form to use it before making the descent similarly in ascent.

STAGE 8A
Rudolfs Hut to Kalser Tauern Haus via the Kalser Tauern

Standard time	4hrs
Ascent	200m
Distance	7km

See map on page 182.

This promenade is an alternative route to the official Runde Tour and is much shorter in duration than the hut connection to the Sudetendeutsche Hut. In poor weather it is an equally fitting way to end the Glockner Rucksack Route. This is a very pleasant journey with good walking without any serious difficulties, though thick mist can prove problematic around the Kalser Tauern pass.

From the Rudolfs Hut follow the route description to the Kalser Tauern pass and descend to Erdiges Eck, to the **signpost** and junction of paths leading to the Sudetendeutsche Hut and Route 517. Continue now south on Route 711, keeping to the left side of the Seebach, east, following the trail through varying types of ground: rocks, boulders and vegetation, with the Dorfer See glacial lake clearly in view (1hr).

> ### THE DORFER SEE
>
> The area around the Dorfer See is particularly fine, with its house-sized boulders and large populations of marmots. This, coupled to the contrast of the quaintness of the Kalser Tauern Haus after the extravagance of the Rudolfs Hut, restores one's soul to the traditions of *gemutlichkeit*.

From the lake, the trail twists and turns for the best part of an hour to negotiate some huge house-sized boulders, making one grateful of not being around when they came tumbling down, before gradually giving way to the delights of the forest and onto the very pleasant Kalser Tauern Haus.

STAGE 9
Sudetendeutsche Hut to Matrei in Ost Tyrol

Standard time	3½–4hrs
Distance	7km
Ascent	Negligible, mostly downhill

From the hut, pick up Route 514 heading southwest down the Aussere Steiner Alm, following a long series of zigzags to the foot of the materials *seilbahn* for the hut at 2012m (¾hr).

From here the path levels out into a graded track that progress through pleasant forest scenery to the farm at Steiner Alm (1909m) (½hr). Good retrospective view up the valley to the Sudetendeutsche Hut.

From the alm you have a choice of two routes, one short one long. The shortest continues as Route 514 and goes via meadows and forest trails through the Aussere Wald forest to the car park on the Tauern Tal main road from where you can walk down the road to Matrei, wait for the post bus or phone for a taxi at the cafeteria (1½hrs).

STAGE 9 – SUDETENDEUTSCHE HUT TO MATREI IN OST TYROL

For a more scenic route follow the signs for Matrei. From the alm follow the path south to the footbridge over the Steinerbach river following the obvious trail through the forest to a clearing with high alpine meadows at 1952m. Proceed along the very pleasant Edelweisswiese Weg, with excellent views toward the Gross Venediger and aerial views of Matrei for half an hour so, to a signpost directing you south to Matrei through the Ranzwald forest to the road and car park at Maschgl (1¼hrs).

Thereafter continue down the road, making short cuts when you can across the hairpin bends, through pretty clusters of alpine chalet style farms and houses to eventually reach the main road at Hinterburg, followed by a 10mins walk into Matrei (1hr).

Bus Service

The bus terminus in Matrei is opposite the Hotel Sport at the entrance to the Virgental valley. The bus timetable is displayed in the hallway at the Sudetendeutsche Hut.
For Innsbruck details are:
- bus from Matrei to Kitzbuhel departs 13:45hrs and arrives 15:03hr.
- train from Kitzbuhel to Innsbruck departs 15:19hrs and arrives 16:26hrs.

HUT DIRECTORY

Unseasonable weather for Climbers Club member Len Reilly

HOHE TAUERN MOUNTAIN HUTS

Salm Hut

The hut descriptions given here are derived from the Austrian Alpine Club (OeAV)'s green Hut Book as well as information from various tourist offices and information published by the huts themselves. Other comments and observations are entirely those of the author.

As more and more of the huts develop websites and email addresses, readers can now book online and check for up-to-date information on many of the huts by visiting: www.aacuk.org.uk, www.alpenverein.at, or www.bergsteigen.at/de/huttendetail.aspx.

ABBREVIATIONS	
B	Bedrooms
M	*Matratzenlager*, dormitory-style accommodation
N	*Notlager*, the winter room or other available space more commonly known as 'sleeping with the furniture'.

Trekking in Austria's Hohe Tauern

Badener Hut (2608m)

Owner	OeAV-S Baden
Location	Situated on a rocky platform at the head of the Frosnitztal valley
Open	Early July to the end of September
Facilities	15B/45M This is a very friendly and well-managed hut having all the necessary rustic charm with creaking of timbers and comfortable rooms.
	Small but excellent choice of local meals with the option of a cooked breakfast.
Valley and Hut Connections	Matreier Tauern Haus 5hrs. Bonn Matreier Hut via Galten Scharte (2884m) 6hrs. Alte and Neue Prager Hut via Loebbentorl (2770m) 3hrs
Address	Genovefa Fuetsch Badener Huette Mittledorf 88 A9972 Virgen Austria
Telephone	0043 (0) 6649 155666
Email	n/a
Website	n/a

The Badener is a relatively high hut with a commanding view over the Frosnitztal valley.

Named after Baden, a town close to Vienna, the hut was constructed in 1911 with extensions added in 1962/70–71 then, refurbished in 1983.

Toilet facilities are a little limited for the size of the hut. There are showers but these are only available when the sun shines to fuel the solar panels.

Badener Hut

No drying room as such but a novel airing cupboard is located on the staircase landing.

The hut is strategically located for crossing the high glaciated massif of the Gross Venediger and hut connection to the Defregger Haus. Those contemplating crossing the Galten Scharte from the Badener Hut should note that this approach is not ideal since much height is lost early in the day: this, together with the fact that crossing the Galten Scharte is a grotty affair at the best of times and varies from year to year, hence the signs outside the hut which state that it is for the experienced only.

BIRNLUCKEN HUT (RIFUGIO BRIGATA TRIDENTINA) 2441M

Owner	CAI Sektion Bruneck
Location	Located on a rocky platform on a subsidiary ridge of the Grasleitenschneid at the head of the Ahrntal valley
Open	Early July to the end of September
Facilities	20B/30M Large *matratzenlager* (sleeping platform) in roof which gets crowded. Good restaurant and toilet facilities but limited when the hut is full.
Valley and Hut Connections	To Kasern in the Ahrntal valley. Warnsdorfer Hut 4hrs. Krimmler Tauern Haus 4hrs. Richter Hut 8hrs. Plauener Hut 8hrs.
Address	Herr Arthur Untergassmair Birnlucken Huette Kirchdorf 80 I-39030 Pretau-Ahrntal Valle Aurina Italy
Telephone	Hut: 0039 (0) 4746 54140 Valley: 0039 (0) 4746 54101 or 552217
Email	knappenhof@dnet.it
Website	n/a

Built in 1890, the hut is one of a quartet of local huts (the others are Warnsdorfer, Neuegergersdorfer and Zittauer), credited to Friedrich Ernst Berger, the *geschaftsfuehrer* of Sektion Warnsdorf.

The present *huttenwirt*, Arthur Untergassmair, has been in charge of the hut since it was rebuilt in the 1970s: in fact it was he who was largely responsible for the rebuilding.

It is interesting that the hut has the same name as a famous *Via Ferrata* route near the Pisciadu Hut in the Sella Group of the Dolomites, except in this case there is no bridge, unless the Birnlucke pass above the hut is seen as a bridge between Austria and Italy.

The history of the hut is similar to all the other huts on the Austrian–Italian border with the South Tyrol, which were forfeited to Italy in 1919 at the end of the First World War. The Birnlucken was no different as it occupies an ancient trade route for the communities of the Ahrntal travelling into the Venediger and beyond. Not surprisingly the Italian army occupied the hut for many years and when they did vacate it in the late 1960s it was in a ruinous state.

Birnlucken Hut with the Birnlucken pass immediately behind the hut

BONN MATREIER HUT 2750M

Owner	DAV-S Bonn
Location	Situated on a rocky platform overlooking the Nilltal valley
Open	Early July to the end of September
Facilities	13B/40M/8N
Valley and Hut Connections	Virgen and Obermauern 3hrs. Badener Hut via Galten Scharte (2884m) 5–6hrs. Eissee Hut 3½hrs. Johannis Hut 7hrs.
Address	Heinz Wolfgang Bonn Matreier Huette Auerfeld 7b A-9971 Matrei Ost Tyrol Austria

Hut Directory – Defregger Haus

Telephone	0043 (0) 6508 209913
Email	Oeav.matrei.ost Tyrol@aon.at
Website	www.alpenverein.at

This is good hut with a commanding view across the Virgental and the distant peaks of Slovenia.

This substantial three storey stone building was built in 1932 by the Austrian OeAV Matrei Sektion and the German DAV Bonn Sektion then enlarged in 1981/84 to its present size. The dining room is particularly pleasant when the light from the setting sun streams through the windows to bathe the room in golden light.

Bonn Matreier Hut

For those interested in 'huts' the Bonn Sektion's other hut, the Bonner Hut is located in the Karnten region of southern Austria in the Goldberg Group not far from Spittal.

Excursions from the hut are rather limited as the hut is very much a one stop shop.

Crossing the Galten Scharte 2884m is a grotty affair due to the unstable nature of the rock on both sides of the Scharte hence the cautionary sign outside the hut which warns for the experienced only.

Defregger Haus (2962m)

Owner Private	*OeTK* (Austrian Tourist Club Vienna)
Location	Situated on a level platform above Mullwitzkopf and the edge of the Mullwitz Kees glacier
Open	Early July to end September
Facilities	35B/60M Good restaurant and toilet facilities but overall can feel cramped and claustrophobic when busy.

Valley and Hut Connections	Pragraten/Hinterbichl 5hrs. Johannis Hut 3hrs. Badener Hut 4hrs. Eissee Hut 3hrs.
Approach	Since the service road now extends as far as the Johannis Hut it is sensible to make use of the jeep taxi service available from Venediger Taxis in Hinterbichl. Tel 0043 (0) 4877 5231 or 5369.
Address	Familie Klaunzer Peter Defregger Haus Edenweg 7 A9971 Matrei in Ost-Tyrol Austria
Telephone	0043 (0) 6769 439145
Email	defreggerhaus@aon.at
Website	n/a

Large three storey hut clad in timber shingles with accommodation for one hundred people. This is the highest hut in the region and the best placed for excursions around the Gross Venediger, which means the hut is always busy and is something of a zoo with all manner of humanity coming and going. However, despite this it remains a pleasant hut with commanding views over the Mullwitz Kees glacier toward the Gross Geiger, Drei Herrn Spitz and Simony Spitz groups.

Built in 1888 by the Austrian Tourist Club (*OeTK*) the hut was subsequently enlarged in 1925 to meet the demands of spring-time skiers, much to the detriment of the Johannis Hut.

EISSEE HUT (2520M)

Owner	Private
Location	Built into the hillside of the Grubachhoehe
Open	Early June to mid October
Facilities	14B/31M Adequate but limited restaurant and toilet facilities.
Valley and Hut Connections	Pragraten 3hrs. Bonn Matreier Hut 3hrs. Johannis Hut via the Zopat Scharte (2955m) 3hrs. Defregger Haus 3hrs.

HUT DIRECTORY – ERZHERZOG JOHANN HUT

Address	Herr Gotthard Bstieler
	Eissee Huette
	St Andra 40
	A-9974 Pragraten
	Oest Tyrol
	Austria
Telephone	Hut 0039 (0) 6644 606459
	Valley 0039 (0) 4877 5323
Email	bstieler@untanet.at
Website	www.eissee.cjb.com
	www.virgentaler.huetten.at

This pleasant little two storey timber hut occupies a strategic position between the Johannis Hut and Bonn Matreier Hut and provides an alternative way to the Defregger Haus via the Wallhorner Torl (3045m).

Eissee Hut

ERZHERZOG JOHANN HUT (ADLERSRUHE) (3454M)

Owner	OeAK Alpine Club
Location	Situated on a platform hewn from the rocks at the junction of the Gross Glockner's south and southeast ridge, the Salmkamp
Open	Early July to the end of September
Facilities	230M, matratzenlager only. There are 10 beds but these are reserved for guides. Good but basic restaurant facilities.

Valley and Hut Connections	Note that there are no easy valley or hut connections from the Adlersruhe, all routes either involve steep rock or glacier crossings or both. Studl Hut 2hrs, Salm Hut 3hrs, Glockner Haus 6hrs, Glorer Hut 3hrs, Oberwalder Hut 8hrs.
Address	Herr Rupert Tembler Erzherzog Johann Hutte Grossdorf 61 A 9981 Kals am Glockner Austria
Telephone	Hut 0043 (0) 4876 8500 or 0664 923 7030 Valley 0043 (0) 4876 8444
Email	info@erzherzog-johann-huette.at adlersruhe@tyrol.com
Website	www.erzherzog-johann-huette.at

Very basic but clean toilet facilities of the long drop variety. The limited water supply is required exclusively for kitchen use which means there are no washrooms. Ensure you take wet wipes with you or be prepared to use the large rain water butt outside or go dirty.

Substantial two storey building with walls covered in timber shingles and windows fitted with brightly painted shutters, the hut is the main base for climbing on the Gross Glockner though the Salm Hut would argue otherwise, as that hut provides the shortest way to the summit of the highest mountain in Austria.

Erzherzog Johann Hut with Gross Glockner in the background

Aptly named the Eagles Rest, the Adlersruhe is the highest hut in Austria and is quintessentially a climber's hut, as most folks staying at the hut will either climb the Gross Glockner or traverse it from some direction. Not surprisingly there are extensive views from the hut and while basic the hut is comfortable for the short time you will stay there.

The Erzherzog Johann Hut at Adlersruhe is named after the Archduke Johann.

Essener Rostocker Hut (2208m)

Owner	DAV-S Essen and Main Spessart
Location	Located on a rocky promontory at the head of the Maurertal valley
Open	Mid June to the end of September
Facilities	49B/70M Drying Room. Good restaurant and toilet facilities and token operated showers.
Valley and Hut Connections	Streden 3hrs, Kursinger Hut via Maurertorl (3108m) 8hrs, Warnsdorfer Hut via Maurertorl 5hrs, Johannis Hut via Turmljoch (2790m) 4hrs.
Approach	See introductory notes for transport details From Matrei take the local bus service from the Sports Haus Hotel to Hinterbichl then taxi to Streden (Venediger Taxi 0039 (0) 4877 5369) and onto the materials/goods hoist (*seilbahn*) at Goeriacher Alm (1459m), from where the field telephone can be used to call the hut. Rucksacks can then be placed in the hoist to allow a rucksack free walk to the hut (1½hrs).
Address	Friedl Steiner Essener Rostocker Huette Iselweg II A-9974 Pragraten Ost Tyrol Austria
Telephone	Hut 0043 (0) 4877 5101 Valley 0043 (0) 4877 5473
Email	info@essener-rostockerhuette.at
Website	www.essener-rostockerhuette.at

This is a massive hut by anyone's description.

The hut(s) occupy an important position for excursions along the Austrian-Italian border, particularly the none-too-easy Drei Herrn Spitz (3498m), the close at hand Malham Spitz (3373m) and the popular Simony Spitz (3488m).

It is also a bit of an odd hut which should be perhaps renamed the odd couple. The hut first started life in 1912 as the Rostocker Hut, the smaller obvious stone building built in the traditional style of hut architecture with communal areas on the ground floor, bedrooms on the first floor and the *matratzenlager* in the roof.

The Essen Sektion's ownership has been fraught with anxiety and despair. Their first hut was in the South Tyrol and was forfeited to the Italians in 1919 at the end of the First World War. Their second hut (1928) in the west of the Venediger near the Umbal Kees glacier was avalanched in 1937. Undeterred a third hut was built in 1939 as the Philip Reuter Hut; this too was destroyed by avalanche. Both these hut ruins are still visible should you have the fortune to pass between the Clara Hut and across the Ahrntal valley into Italy. The Essen Sektion, having now given up hope of owning their own hut, agreed with the Rostock Sektion, who at that time were more or less broke and unable to finance the modernisation and extension of the Rostocker Hut, that they would build the Essener Hut next to the Rostocker Hut to be known as the Essener Rostocker Hut.

Essener Rostocker Hut, with the Simony Group and Maurertorl on the horizon

And so in 1962 the very substantial and less pleasing four storey Essener Hut was built linking the two buildings together to provide much-needed expansion, generally for the benefit of ski touring enthusiasts.

THE VILLAGE OF FUSCH

Fusch is a typical small Austrian village located on the main road linking the towns of Kaprun, Zell am See and Heiligenblut via the Glocknerstrasse. The village has a church, a few shops, hotels and guest houses.

If you have not secured accommodation, the author can recommend the Landgasthof Wasserfall. The gasthof is more of a hotel than a guest house providing full accommodation with bar and restaurant service. The gasthof is located on the main road and is close to the path, signpost indicating the way to the Gleiwitzer Hut.

Contact	Landgasthof Wasserfall
	Familie Hollaus
	A 5672 Fusch a.d. Glocknerstrasse
	Austria

Telephone	0043 (0) 6546 249
Email	Fusch@Gasthof-Wasserfall.at
Website	www.gasthof-wasserfall.at

GLEIWITZER HUT (2174M)

Owner	DAV *Sektion Tittmoning*
Location	Situated on a level platform at the head of the Edelweisskopferl buttress with commanding views to the Hoher Dachstein and further east to Austria's Dolomites, the Tennen Gebirge
Open	Mid June to early October
Facilities	19B/53M/12N Modest but adequate toilet and restaurant facilities.
Valley and Hut Connections	Fusch 4hrs, Kaprun 5hrs, Heinrich Schwaiger Haus via Kempsenkopf (3090m) 8–10hrs.
Address	Herr Erich Brugger Gleiwitzer Huette Zeller Fusch 142 A 5672 Fusch Austria
Telephone	Hut (0043) 0676 478 3420 Valley (0043) 0676 3921381
Email	e-brugger@sbg.at
Website	www.gleiwitzerhuette.at

Another casualty of politics and war, the hut is named after the northern German town of Gleiwitz in Silesia which is now in Poland.

Built in 1900 with few changes over the years, ownership was transferred from the DAV Gleiwitz Sektion to the Bavarian Sektion of Tittmoning in 1968. Previous to that the hut had a chequered history; during the First World War when the hut was closed it was frequently used by army deserters trying to escape the carnage of war. After the Second World War the hut was re-named the Hoch Tenn

TREKKING IN AUSTRIA'S HOHE TAUERN

Hut and ownership passed between the various *sektions* of Zell am See, Amstetten and Rohrbach Muel Kries.

This is a very pleasant hut in the *gemutlichkeit* tradition and one of the best huts on the Glockner Rucksack Route and Runde Tour.

Gleiwitzer Hut

GLOCKNER HAUS ALPINCENTER (2132M)

Owner	OeAV Sektion Klagenfurt
Location	Located on the roadhead of the Glockner Strasse road high above the Margaritzen stausee reservoir
Open	Early May to the end of October
Facilities	48B/40M First class accommodation and everything you would expect of a hotel
Valley and Hut Connections	Heiligenblut 3hrs, Salm Hut 3hrs, Oberwalder Hut 3hrs, Fusch 6–7hrs
Address	Herr Johann Krobath Alpincenter Glocknerhaus A 9844 Heiligenblut Ost Tyrol Austria
Telephone	Hut 0043 (0) 4824 24666 Valley 0043 (0) 3533 246
Email	info@glocknerhaus.com
Website	www.glocknerhaus.com

Built in 1875–76 on the initiative of two post masters, Winklern Molltal and Lorenz Wernisch. Unfortunately the initial project ran out of money. Cash eventually came when one or both of them had the brainwave to raise funds by holding a lottery to complete the building. The hut was extended in 1885, then extensively enlarged in 1926–27 to its present size when an additional storey was added.

Because of the First World War and the depression that followed, the hut was forced to close in 1929. Sadly it was then vandalised, suffered avalanche damage and was more or less abandoned in the years leading up to the Second World War. At the end of the Second World War in 1945 the British Army occupied the hut as a base for mountain training of officers. Patched up the hut eventually reopened in 1948, was totally refurbished in 1964 and again in 1995 when the sun terrace was added.

Glockner Haus with Gross Glockner in the clouds

The outside terrace has a number of murals that depict the history of the Pasterzen Kees glacier which sadly has all but disappeared from the environs of the hut, in total contrast to the mid 1800s when it was within stepping distance of the hut's front door. This is a good hut and a splendid place to be before picking up the rucksack once more to head into the mountains.

GLORER HUT (2651M)

Owner	DAV Sektion Eichstatt
Location	Situated on the path junction of the Bergertorl an old trade route between Kals and the remote villages to the north
Open	Early June to mid October
Facilities	10B/40M/4N
Valley and Hut Connections	Kals 4hrs, Luckner Haus 2hrs, Salm Hut 2hrs, Studl Hut 3hrs, Glockner Haus 5hrs
Address	Herr Anton Rieple Glora Huette Unterpeisschlach 2 A 9981 Kals am Gross Glockner Austria

Telephone	Hut 0043 (0) 6643 032200
	Valley 0043 (0) 4876 8566
Email	toni@aon.net
Website	www.dav-eichstaett.de

Named after the small hamlet of Glor just above Kals, the hut was built by local guides in 1887. Enlarged over the years the present three storey stone built hut follows the traditions of the time and is almost a mirror image of the Salm Hut.

Although the author has no personal knowledge of the hut since I have had no reason to go there, I am reliably informed the hut is welcoming in the gemutlichkeit tradition.

HEINRICH SCHWAIGER HAUS (2802M)

Owner	DAV Sektion Munchen
Location	On the west side of the Unterer Fochezkopfes high above the Mooserboden Stausee hydroelectric reservoir
Open	Mid June to the end of September
Facilities	17B/68M Basic toilet facilities due to the limited water supply. Modest restaurant service. *Seilbahn lift* facility for hoisting rucksacks to the hut available from the Mooserboden dam wall
Valley and Hut Connections	Mooserboden 2hrs, Oberwalder Hut 6hr, Gleiwitzer Hut 8 to 10hrs; Rudolfs Hut 7 to 8hr
Address	Herr Ferdinand Treffner
	Heinrich Schweiger Haus
	Mooseboden
	A 5710 Kaprun
	Austria
Telephone	Hut 0043 (0) 6547 8662; 0043 (0) 6645 168862
	Valley 0043 (0) 8021 506756
Email	f.treffner@GMX.at
Website	www.alpenverein-muenchen.de
	www.heinrich-schwaiger-haus.at

HUT DIRECTORY – HOFMANNS HUT

While not strictly on the official Glockner Runde Tour, the main reason for visiting this hut is to climb the Grosses Weisbachhorn or to make the glacier traverse to or from the Oberwalder Hut. This is a high hut with extensive views in all directions.

The original hut, built in 1872, was named the Albert Kaindl Hut after a prominent

Heinrich Schwaiger Haus

member of Sektion Linz. Located at a slightly lower level than the present hut, the old hut was a simple lean-to structure built into the cliff face that soon started to disintegrate due to changes in the permafrost and quite simply fell apart. By 1895 ownership had passed from Sektion Linz to the wealthier Sektion Muenchen who committed themselves to building a new hut.

The second hut on the present site was opened in 1902 and is named after Heinrich Schwaiger, a D and OeAV pioneer and committee member who sadly died of pneumonia the day before the hut was opened. His portrait is proudly displayed in the main *gaste stube* (dining room). That hut also fell apart mostly due to neglect during the war years and became unusable by the early 1950s. Sektion Muenchen then decided a more robust hut should be built. Opened in 1956, the third and present hut is a two-storey rather elongated affair and, without being unkind, is a bland, metal-clad tin shed. Inside, however, is the traditional rustic feel of timber panelling with the gaste stube split into an expandable dining room to conserve heat while the first floor has nice-sized bedrooms for two, three and four persons, with the rest of the space given to *matratzenlager*.

This is a good no frills hut in the mountaineering tradition of providing the basic needs of food and shelter.

HOFMANNS HUT (2444M)

Owner	OeAV Akademische. Vienna
Location	Situated on the hillside of the Gamsgrube, the hut was strategically positioned for excursions on the north side of the Gross Glockner during the mountain's golden era as

	the Pasterzen Kees glacier in 1800 reached the level of the present day Gamsgrubenweg footpath and tourist trail
Open	Presently closed with no indication of when it will reopen.
Facilities	16B/50M/20N
Telephone	Hut 0043 (0) 4824 2575 Valley 0043 (0) 5285 6250

Named after Karl Hofmann, friend both of royalty and of Johann Studl of Studl hut fame, the original stone bivvy shelter was used as a base by the Archduke Johann for shooting gams (antelope) on the slopes of the Gamsgrube, hence its name.

Built in 1860 with extensions in 1869–1870, largely from funds by Hofmann and the Heiligenblut guides it was again extended in 1887 at Studl's expense when ownership was transferred to the DOeAV Prague.

Thereafter it was transferred to OeAV Vienna in 1911; they extended the hut to its present size in 1930.

Sadly for whatever reason the hut has slid into decline which has led to more rain and snow being driven into the hut, accelerating the freeze-thaw process that it has now been forced to close.

The latest news is that ownership is in the process of being transferred to the Klagenfurt Sektion whom have declared their intention is to re-build this historic hut, that enjoys one of the best views from any hut terrace in the Eastern Alps and is a fitting memorial of Karl Hofmann who was killed in action in 1871, and restore it to its former glory.

JOHANNIS HUT (2121M)

Owner	DAV-S Oberland
Location	Situated in a bowl carved by retreating glaciers at the head of the Dorfertal valley.
Approach	Taxi service to and from Kals 0664 521 9089 or walking the 8km of paved road or forest tracks
Open	Early June to the end of September.

Hut Directory – Johannis Hut

Facilities	50M No beds but tastefully fitted out matratzenlager compartmentalised into bunks of two and three. Good restaurant and toilet facilities with hot water on tap.
Valley and Hut Connection	Hinterbichl 2½hrs. Defregger Haus 1½hrs. Bonn Matreier Hut via Zopat Scharte (2955m) and Eissee Hut 7hrs. Badener Hut via Frosnitztorl 5hrs. Kursinger Hut via Obersulzbachtorl (2921m) 5hrs. Essen-Rostocker Hut via Turmljoch (2790m) 4hrs.
	Jeep service available from Hinterbichl bus stop.
	Taxi service available from Venediger Taxis 0043 (0) 4877 5369
Address	Herr Leonard Unterwurzacher
	Johannis Huette Hinterbichl 19/A A-9974 Pragraten Ost Tyrol Austria
Telephone	Hut 0043 (0) 4877 5150 Valley 0043 (0) 4877 5387
Email	info@johannishuette.at
Website	www.johannishuette.at

This superb little hut has the distinction of being the oldest hut in the Venediger Group, and is named after the Austrian Archduke John.

Construction of the hut was funded by the Archduke with work commencing in 1857, but as so often happens with funds that are gifted the money ran out before the hut could be completed. The hut then fell into disrepair until it was

Johannis Hut

acquired by the OeAV in 1871, who gave it to the Prague Sektion to manage in 1876. The Prague Sektion then set about basic repairs to the hut to make it usable which it managed to do successfully for a few years until the hut lost its strategic importance as a base for climbing the high peaks when the better-placed, privately-owned Defregger Haus opened in 1890.

The hut was extended in 1930 and totally refurbished in 2006 but retains the quintessential style of the period with just two storeys and a steep, pitched roof to shed snow. Walls are clad with larch shingles that have darkened with the passing of time, providing a nice rustic quality. Everything about the hut has an excellent homely feel to it and adequately illustrates the meaning of the word *gemutlichkeit*.

While not as high as the Defregger Haus the hut maintains a strategic position for excursions into the high mountains and is better placed for some hut-to-hut connections.

KALSER TAUERN HAUS (1754M)

Owner	DAV-S Moenchengladbach
Location	In a forest clearing at the upper edge of the Dorfertal valley.
Open	Mid-June to the end of September
Facilities	20B/28M
Valley and Hut Connections	Kals 3hrs. Rudolfs Hut via Kalser Tauern (2513m) 4hrs. Sudetendeutsche Hut via Gradez Sattel (2826m) 7–8hrs.
Address	Frau Gerlinde Gilber Kals Tauernhaus Lana 9 A 9981 Kals Austria
Telephone	Hut 0043 (0) 663 857090 Valley 0043 (0) 4876 8393
Email	peter.gliber@aon.at
Website	www.alpenverein-mg.de www.kalser-tauernhaus.de

Splendid stone-built four-storey hut in the old traditional style with windows fitted with brightly painted shutters.

While popular with day-trippers from Kals it is not unusual to have the run of the place once the sun has gone down.

HUT DIRECTORY – KRIMMLER TAUERN HAUS

Kalser Tauern Haus

Constructed in 1928–30, with funds raised by the Kals Bergfuehrer Association, thereafter it was transferred to the Moenchengladbach Sektion of the DAV in 1962.

The hut had a lucky escape in the late 1960s when plans to build a hydroelectric dam that would have left the hut under 40m of water were thwarted.

The hut has that nice cosy feeling of *gemutlichkeit* about it, with creaking timbers and timber-panelled walls with scenes from the northern German town of Moenchengladbach. This is a lovely hut and an ideal family venue where children can roam freely through the forest.

KRIMMLER TAUERN HAUS (1631M)

Owner	Private
Location	Located at the head of the Krimmler Achental valley.
Open	May to October
Access	Bus service from Mayrhofen to Krimml 08:30/09:40hrs Taxi service from Krimml to Krimml Tauern Haus 08:45/10:30hrs
Facilities	23B/40M Full restaurant and toilet facilities as can be expected of a hotel. Beds are by reservation only. *Matratzenlager* for 40
Valley and Hut Connections	Krimml 3hrs. Krimml to Warndorfer Hut 5hrs. Richter Hut 4hrs. Zittauer Hut 4–5hrs.
Address	Herr Friedrich Geisler A-5743 Krimml Tyrol Austria
Telephone	0043 (0) 6564 8327
Email	info@krimmler-tauernhaus.at
Website	www.krimmler-tauernhaus.at

A delightful old farmhouse that has its origins in the 14th century, farming the very fertile glacial basin and alp around the hut, providing that quintessential definition of chalets and all things alpine.

Apart from farming, the hut was built in the Middle Ages as a hospice to provide shelter for travellers crossing the main ranges over the Maurertorl into the Venediger and Virgental valleys and across the Krimml Tauern into the Ahrntal valley.

Krimmler Tauern Haus

The hut itself is very pleasant with some interesting memorabilia in the 'alte gaste stubl' of life on the farm, particularly photographs of cattle drives into the Ahrntal. Visually the hut is very old with smoke stained timber panelling and pictures of various people through the ages.

Unfortunately because the hut is on the well-beaten trail and caters for all and sundry, the service on hand does not match that of the hut's grandeur, having lost the very essence and meaning of the word *gemutlichkeit*. If you have to stay here don't expect any special treatment just because you are *alpenverein*!

KURSINGER HUT (2558M)

Owner	OeAV-S Salzburg
Location	Situated on a prominent knoll at the head of the Obersulzbachtal valley with a magnificent view toward the Gross Venediger (3660m) and Gross Geiger (3360m).
Open	Mid June to the end of September.
Facilities	50B/100M/50N This is a well-appointed hut which is frequently used to train the Austrian national ski team, as such it has excellent all-round facilities including a wholesome menu. Good toilet facilities with hot water and token-operated showers. Drying room.

HUT DIRECTORY – KURSINGER HUT

Valley and Hut Connections	Neukirchen 6hrs. Warnsdorfer via Gams Spitzl (2888m) 8hrs. Neue Prager Hut via Venediger Scharte (3413m) 5hrs. Essener-Rostocker Hut via Maurertorl (3108m) 8hrs.
Address	Monika and Emil Widman Kursinger Huette Sulzau Obersulzbach Markt 90 A 5741 Neukirchen Am Grossvenediger Austria
Telephone	Hut 0043 (0) 6565 6450 Valley 0043 (0) 6549 7986
Email	Josef.Hetz@sbg.at
Website	office@tauernguide.at www.kuersingerhuette.at

This is not so much a hut but a complex of huts that have been built not to meet the demands of climbers but more for skiers and ski teams.

Built in 1885 with subsequent enlargement and adding of annexes in 1926, 1929 and 1938, then built to its present size in 1983. Because of the constant threat of avalanches all the buildings are robustly built of stone.

As with the Johannis and Essener Rostocker Huts' the Kursinger has an interesting history. The hut is named after Ignaz Kursinger, a local politician and magistrate who was an active mountaineer during the early 1800s as the area at that time was

Kursinger Hut with Gross Geiger in the background

the prime route for early excursions on the Gross Venediger around 1830. Not surprisingly many parties would have taken shelter in the various alms huts high up in the Obersulzbachtal valley or would have camped or bivouacked near to the site of the present day hut, bearing in mind that the Obersulzbach Kees glacier would have reached far down the valley and beyond the site of the present day hut.

Kursinger eventually climbed the mountain in 1841, taking with him an entourage of 45 people, comprising a motley bunch of porters, guides, farm workers and friends all of whom are depicted in an illustration in the alte *gaste stubl* along with a portrait of Kursinger himself. 26 of the group got to the top while the rest faded away exhausted on the glacier. One man in the group who stood out was Anton Rohregger, a forester who with Kursinger had explored the route over a period of 20 years, managing to fulfil his dream, with Kursinger, at the age of 68.

The year after, Rohregger built a small hut somewhere near the site of the present day hut(s) which he named Kursinger. Not surprisingly because of Rohregger's age the little hut soon fell into a ruinous state until the Salzburg Sektion took possession in 1875. They then commenced rebuilding and enlarging the hut. This too fell into disrepair and was abandoned until 1885 when they built an entirely new hut.

Which of the huts is the original hut I don't know but as you sit outside on the terrace, try to imagine Kursinger and Rohregger with their entourage, an assorted mix of society, setting out for the summit of the Gross Venediger 150 years ago fully provisioned with wine, bread, cheese and a bugler to sound the expedition's success when they reached the top.

Sir Martin Conway also passed this way, becoming snowbound in August 1894 when they partied, celebrating the Emperor Franz Josef's birthday with champagne in good style. Splendid indeed.

> Should you have the misfortune to be caught out in bad weather while at the Kursinger Hut and decide to descend, you should weigh your decision carefully as the Obersulzbach valley is exceedingly long and does not present an easy journey out of the mountains.
>
> From the hut descend to the little hamlet at Posch-Berndl Alm (3hrs) from where you can hire a taxi. A 20mins ride will then place you on the main road from where you can get the local bus service to either Mittersill and Innsbruck or over the Gerlos Pass to Mayrhofen.
>
> If you undertake this journey you will understand why it took Kursinger and Rohregger such a long time to explore the upper reaches of the Obersulzbachtal valley as a gateway to the Gross Venediger.

LUCKNER HAUS (1984M)

Owner	Private
Location	Situated at the road head above Kals midway up the Koednitztal valley and starting point for most routes on the Gross Glockner. Car park and bus terminal for Kals, Huben, Matrei
Open	Early March to the end of October.
Facilities	32B/21M. Everything necessary you would expect from a hotel.
Valley and Hut Connections	See approach notes. Regular local bus service from Kals with connections from Lienz and Kitzbuhel via Huben. Kals 1½hr. Luckner Hut 1hr. Studl Hut 2½ to 3hr. Glorer Hut 2hr
Address	Herr Johann Oberlohr Lucknerhaus Hotel Tscheltsch 2 A-9653 Liesing Austria
Telephone	0043 (0) 4876 8555 or (0) 4876 8277
Email	lucknerhaus@tirol.com
Website	www.tiscover.com/lucknerhaus

The Luckner Haus is a very old guest house-cum-hotel, often packed with day-trippers who come to see 'the mountain'. A pleasant-looking building in typical alpine chalet style, with a classic view of the Gross Glockner. Those with sharp eyes will also be able to pick out the Adlersruhe and Eagles Rest hut high on the mountain.

LUCKNER HUT (2241M)

Owner	Private
Location	Situated just off the main track en-route to the Studl and Glorer Huts.
Open	Early July to the end of September

Facilities	12B/23M
Valley and Hut Connections	Kals 2½hr. Luckner Haus 1hr. Studl Hut. 1½ to 2hr. Glorer Hut 2hr. Salm Hut 3hr. Baggage transfer available from the Luckner Haus.
Address	Florian Oberlohr Luckner Hutte Glor 1 A-9981 Kals Austria
Telephone	Hut 0043 (0) 4876 8455 Valley 0043 (0) 4876 8221
Email	lucknerhof@tirol.com
Website	www.tiscover.com/lucknerhuette

The hut was rebuilt in the 1960s to replace the original hut which was largely destroyed by an avalanche some years earlier. A pleasant three-storey hut, with excellent views of the Gross Glockner, the hut's main business is providing refreshment for visitors who have made the effort to undertake the 1hr walk from the Luckner Haus and those climbers returning from the Glockner wanting a quick beer.

OBERWALDER HUT (2973M)

Owner	OeAV-S Austria
Location	Situated on a rocky platform on the south ridge of the Grosser Bergstall overlooking a sea of glaciers with a commanding view of the Gross Glockner and the pointed peak of the Johannisberg (3463m).
Open	End of June to the end of september
Facilities	46B/63M/30N Good toilet facilities but limited use due to water restrictions. Token-operated showers when water is available. Good restaurant service, often buffet-style evening meal and breakfast.

HUT DIRECTORY – OBERWALDER HUT

Valley and Hut Connections	Heiligenblut via Glockner Haus 6hrs. Rudolfs Hut via Odenwinkel Scharte (3233m) 7–8hrs. Heinrich Schwaiger Haus 6hrs. Salm Hut 6–7hrs.
Address	Herr Wolfgang Hackel Oberwalder Huette Seeuferstrasse 6b A-5700 Zellam See Austria
Telephone	Hut 0043 (0) 4824 2546 Valley 0043 (0) 6542 4700
Email	info@alpinsport.at
Website	www.oberwalderhuette.at

Named after the hat manufacturer Thomas Oberwalder, a farmer's son from St Jakob in the neighbouring Defregger valley. Thomas was an active climber throughout the Dolomites but was more famous for his daring solo ascents of the Matterhorn, Mont Blanc and Jungfrau. Sadly he was killed in a huge avalanche on his way to the Hofmanns Hut on 3 March 1906. The search party found him mortally injured two days later.

Oberwalder Hut with Gross Glockner in the background

Built in 1905 and opened in 1908, the hut was used to train Alpine troops during the First World War, which led to it being refurbished in 1920. Thereafter the hut was extended in 1923, 1926 and 1929, and then again to its present size in 1985.

The Oberwalder is a very pleasant three-storey hut, clad in timber shingles that have been scorched and stained with the passing of time.

The ground floor has the usual dining room with a number of individual *stubls* for more intimate occasions or formal use. This is a very good hut and worthy of a visit.

Plauener Hut (2363m)

Owner	DAV-S Plauen Vogtland
Location	Situated on a rocky platform on the western slopes of the Richter Spitze.
Open	Mid June to End September.
Access	Bus service from Mayrhofen to Zillergrund Stausee 08:30/09:30/10:30/11:30/12:30/14:30/15:30hrs
Facilities	74M No bedrooms as such but the *matratzenlager* are tastefully fitted out into rooms for five, seven and nine occupants. Good restaurant and toilet facilities including token-operated showers. Drying room.
Valley and Hut Connections	Local bus service to and from Mayrhofen. Richter Hut via Gams Scharte 3½hrs; via Zillerplatten Scharte 6–7hrs. Birnlucken Hut 7–8hrs.
Address	Frau Gisela Eiter Plauener Huette A6426 Roppen Nr 135 Austria
Telephone	Hut 0043 (0) 6502 250369 Valley 0043 (0) 5417 5167
Email	plauenerhuette@telering.at
Website	www.plauenerhuette.de.vu

Named after the city of Plauener in Voegtland, the hut was built in collaboration with the Austrian and German Alpine Clubs in 1898 then extended through the years 1912, 1925 and 1958, then more latterly in 1998 when it was refurbished to its present size as part of the hut's centenary celebrations.

A relatively large three-storey building with traditional timber panelled walls in the dining room to provide that homely feel. The dining room walls are adorned by pictures of dignitaries long deceased, while more practical memorabilia chair plaques dedicated to past members.

The main excursions from the hut are the Reichen Spitze (3303m), the highest in the group, which provides a good glacier journey and rock scramble to finish. The Wildergerlos Spitze is a tad lower at 3280m but provides a similar climb. You will do well to climb both in a single day's outing!

Hut Directory – Prager Hut (Alte)

Plauener Hut with Kuchelmooskopf on the left, Reichen Spitze on the right

The route to the Richter Hut over the Gams Scharte (2991m) is a bit of a chossy mess and should only be undertaken in good weather by experienced parties. Alternatively take the long way round via the Zillerplatten Scharte (2874m).

Views across the void from the hut are dominated by the Rauchkofel (3252m) (the 'rough/jagged smoking mountain') then back down the valley to the Zillergrundl reservoir in time to reflect that not so long ago just getting to the hut would have been an all-day affair. Since the hydroelectricity plant was constructed in the late 1960s easy access has been provided with the provision of a local bus service. Not surprisingly now that the hut is readily accessible from Mayrhofen it is often packed during the day with visitors from Mayrhofen, however once the sun's gone down it is the mountain traveller that will be found in residence.

Prager Hut (Alte) (2489m)

Owner	DAV-S Oberland
Location	Situated on a rocky spur at the head of the Tauerntal valley
Open	Early July to the end of September.
Facilities	17B/10M Not normally available for overnight stay. Sometimes used as an overspill facility if the Neue Prager Hut is full or when the weather is bad. When open, limited restaurant and toilet facilities.
Valley and Hut Connections	Innergschloss/Venediger Haus 3hrs. Badener Hut via Loebbentorl (2770m) 4hrs. Neue Prager Hut 1hr. Sankt Poltener Hut 6hrs. Neue Further Hut via Sandebentorl (2753m) 5hrs.
Address	See Neue Prager Hut

Prager Hut (Alte)

A super little hut which has been largely superseded due to its close proximity to the Neue Prager Hut.

Constructed in 1872 and severely damaged by avalanche in 1877 the hut was built as close to the Schlaten Kees glacier as was humanly possible in those days, to make it the best-placed hut for mountain excursions on the Gross Venediger and adjacent peaks.

The hut is a simple two-storey stone structure that has served the area well but as the glaciers retreated so the popularity of the hut as a base has declined in favour of the Neue Prager Hut, which is 300m higher and closer to the big peaks.

However, for the mountain traveller who might be passing through the area (as was Sir Martin Conway in 1894) the hut remains a good place to stay without the hustle and bustle of its close neighbour, with its dawn chorus and clamour of souls rushing to get onto the fourth highest mountain in Austria.

PRAGER HUT (NEUE) (2796M)

Owner	DAV-S Oberland
Location	Situated on a prominent ridge of the Hinterer Kesselkopf close to the Schlaten Kees glacier
Open	Early July to the end of September
Facilities	64B/36M Full restaurant and toilet facilities that can be expected from one of the largest hut in the Venediger.
Valley and Hut Connections	Matreier Tauern Haus 5hrs. Innergschloss and Venediger Haus 4hrs. Badener Hut via Loebbentorl (2770m) 4hrs. Kursinger Hut via Venediger Scharte (3414m) 4hrs. Sankt Poltener Hut 7hrs. Neue Thuringer Hut via the Schwarzkopf Scharte (2861m) 7hrs.

HUT DIRECTORY – PRAGER HUT (NEUE)

Address	Tino Mai Neue Prager Huette Postfach 19 A-9971 Matrei Ost Tyrol Austria
Telephone	Hut 0043 (0) 4875 8840 Valley 0043 (0) 7203 47678
Email	info@neue-prager-huette.at
Website	www.neue-prager-huette.at

This hut is huge with accommodation for 100+ people that averages 3500 bed-nights in a typical season. While it's a good base for climbing the local peaks its close proximity to the Gross Venediger means that throughout August it is usually packed to capacity with all manner of folk who wish to climb the mountain. Consequently don't expect to have brilliant service in the *gemutlichkeit* tradition or to have a good night's sleep, but if you enjoy a party then the hut comes highly recommended and is a good place to stay before heading off into the quiet of the mountains. Remember if you are a party of more than four you are advised to book and reserve bed spaces otherwise you are likely to be *notlager*, sleeping with the furniture.

Constructed commenced in 1904 by the OeAV Sektion Prague under the leadership of Johann Studl (see Studl Hut) and his *bergfuehrer* friend Vincent Ganzer, with plans to accommodate 130 people. Completion of the hut was delayed by the usual problems of money and weather. Funds were eventually raised by the ladies committee of the OeAV Sektion Prague to complete the interior and provide furniture and fittings. Once opened the hut was provided with a 'local lady warden' Frau Elise Muelburger who managed the hut along with her husband, *bergfuehrer* Andreas from 1908 to 1945 with a few First World War years missing. Her presence is recorded in a group photograph at Venediger Haus taken at the end of the war in 1946.

Prager Hut (Neue) with Gross Glockner on the right-hand horizon

The Second World War impacted greatly on the OeAV Sektion Prague leaving them with just 30 members due to the dissipation of members expelled by the Czechs in 1946. Membership took off again in the 1950s with the hut being restored to its original state then, when more money was available, was refurbished in 1977. The hut was then enlarged in 1983 to its present size. Thereafter in 1992 ownership was transferred to the DAV Sektion Oberland.

RICHTER HUT (2374M)

Owner	DAV-S Bergfreunde Rheydt (Rhineland)
Location	Situated on a rocky knoll on the eastern slopes of the Rainbach Spitze
Open	Mid June to the end of September
Facilities	10B/40N/16N Adequate but limited restaurant and toilet facilities
Valley and Hut Connections	Krimmler Tauern Haus 2+hr. Zittauer Hut 4hrs. Plauener Hut via Gams Scharte 2991m 4hrs or via the Zillerplatten Scharte 2874m 7hrs. Warnsdorfer Hut 6hrs. Birlucken Hut 7-8hr
Address	Familie Erwin and Burgi Bachmaier Richter Huette A-5743 Krimml 72 Austria
Telephone	Hut 0043 (0) 6564 3704908 Valley 0043 (0) 6564 7328
Email	richterhuette@gmx.at

A superb little hut unspoilt by the passing of time.

The hut was originally constructed as a private hut by Anton Franz Richter in 1896 and run by members of the Richter family well into the 1960s, when management of the hut was transferred to the DAV-S. Anton Richter is buried on the Richter Spitze which bears his name.

The hut is the third hut to be built with the last two occupying the present site. The original hut was built much higher-up at 2623m but was avalanched during the first winter of opening. The second hut which occupies the present site was much bigger being around three times the size of the present hut. This too was avalanched in 1917 leaving the hut as we see it today.

HUT DIRECTORY – RUDOLFS HUT/BERG HOTEL

Richter Hut

The hut is the quintessential visual epitome of what a mountain hut should be, a small two storey building, stone built of stout quality, whose interior has the creaking of timber and panelled walls darkened with age with pictures of the hut through the years. The hut has a genuine welcoming feel about it in the *gemutlichkeit* tradition.

Expeditions from the hut are limited but strategically it is the shortest way to the Plauener Hut over the Gams Scharte (2991m), a route which should only be undertaken in good weather due to the difficult ground on the Plauener Hut side of the col.

Other hut connections include the Zittauer Hut via the Rosskar Scharte (2687m), Birnlucken Hut in the South Tyrol via the Krimmler Tauern (2634m) and the abandoned Neugersdorfer Hut and Krimmler Tauern Haus in the Krimmler Achental valley en route to the Warnsdorfer Hut.

RUDOLFS HUT/BERG HOTEL (2315M)

Owner	Private
Location	Situated on a rocky platform off the Schafbuechel with good views overlooking the man-made Weissee hydroelectricity reservoir towards the Stubacher Sonnblich and Granat Spitze
Open	End of June to the end of October
Facilities	200B/53M 1st class restaurant and toilet facilities as expected of a hotel
Valley and Hut Connections	Uttendorf via cable car 3hrs. Kalser Tauern Haus 4½hrs. Sudetendeutsche Hut 7–8hrs. Gruen See Hut via Karl Fuerst Hut and Granat Scharte (2974m) 8–10hrs.

Address	Geschaftsfuehrer Herr Hans Gregoritsch Berghotel Rudolfs Huette Stubach 82 A-5723 Uttendorf Weissee Pinzgau Austria
Telephone	Hut 0043 (0) 6563 8221 Valley 0043 (0) 6542 788
Email	info@rudolfshuette.at
Website	http://www.alpinzentrum-rudolfshuette.at

Named after Rudolf, Crown Prince of Austria and Hungary, son of Emperor Franz Josef and the beautiful Kaiserin Elisabeth (known as Sisi, the Reluctant Princess) famed for his filmstar good looks but more so for his frustration with court life that ended with Rudolf shooting himself and his lover and mistress at their hunting lodge in the Vienna woods at Mayerling. Clumsily covered up by the Emperor to look like a hunting accident, others say he was murdered for embarrassing the Royal family. The ensuing scandal has been the source of countless books and a Hollywood movie. However for us and despite the name, this is not so much a hut but a mountain hotel presently owned by local hotelier Wilfried Holleis.

Built in 1874 then extended in 1883, 1895, 1922 and right up to the 1950s, when the hydroelectric scheme started with the creation of the Weissee reservoir, which in turn put the site of the original hut under water. This led to a new hut being constructed in 1958 on the present site.

From 1959 onward the OeAV operated the hut as a hotel and then from 1979 it became the national alpine training centre with 200 beds and a further 53 in the dormitory. In 1990 the hut was sold to the DAV who in turn sold it to a private hotelier from Ziller who promptly set about making the hut into the massive complex it is today with 20m climbing wall, swimming pool, sun lounge, bar restaurant etc.

Rudolfs Hut-Berg Hotel with Granat Spitze on the centre skyline, Stubacher Sonnblick to the right and Weiss See reservoir-lake below

Climbs from the hut are limited to the neighbouring peaks particularly the Granatz Spitze (3086m) and Sonnblick (3088m). However, there are a number of good rock climbing crags not too far from the hut and these linked to the glaciers is what made the hut ideal as a training centre.

Today the hut is more popular as a venue for valley-based tourists from Zell am See and Kaprun who come to the hut for a mountain experience viewed from the safe distance of the terrace or sun-lounge.

Despite my quip, it is reasonably priced and a good place to stay if you have had several days on the hill and wish to get cleaned up and relax for a while.

NEUE SAJAT HUT (2600M)

Owner	Private
Location	Situated at the head of the Sajat Mahder couloir
Open	Mid May to the end of October
Facilities	43B/15M Everything that can be expected of a hotel
Valley and Hut Connections	Eissee Hut 2½hrs, Johannis Hut 2½hrs, Bonn Matreier Hut 5hrs
Address	Herr Stefan Kratzer Neue Sajat Huette Bichl 8 A9974 Pragraten am Grossvenediger. Austria
Telephone	0043 (0) 6645 454460
Email	kratzer@netway.at
Website	www.sajathuette.at

This recently reopened hut was built to replace the old hut which was totally destroyed by an avalanche in 2001.

While the author has no personal knowledge of the hut as it is not strictly on the Venediger Hoehenweg I am reliably informed that the hut is well-appointed being more of a hotel than a hut and is dubbed 'the castle in the mountains' no doubt from its turreted gables.

Salm Hut (2644m)

Owner	OeAv *Sektion* Vienna
Location	Situated on a grassy plateau below the Hasenbalfen with a good view of the Gross Glockner and for those with sharp eyes the Adlersruhe hut.
Open	Mid June to the end of September
Facilities	25B/25M Modest restaurant service. Token operated showers available but otherwise cold water only.
Valley and Hut Connections	Luckner Haus 3hrs, Studl Hut 3hrs via the Pfort Scharte (2828m), Glockner Haus 3hrs, Adlersruhe 3½hrs
Address	Frau Helga Pratl Salm Huette Breitenbrunn 3/3 A 8253 Waldbach Austria
Telephone	Hut 0043 (0) 4824 2089 Valley 0043 (0) 6547 11002
Email	salmhuette@aon.at
Website	alpenverein.wien@kabelnet.at

The Salm Hut is an historic hut and has the distinction of being the oldest hut in the Eastern Alps, having occupied three locations. The first hut was built in 1799 from funds provided by Franz Xaver von Salm-Rifferscheidt, Bishop of Gurk. That hut had a commanding view of the Gross Glockner being located at the foot of the then Leiten Kees glacier tucked into the moraines on the 2640m contour. The hut was in every sense of the word a hut comprising a small entrance for cooking and a single room for sleeping just three metres square. Being of timber the hut gradually deteriorated and by 1828 was unfit for use. This led the Klagenfurt Sektion to commence construction of the second hut at the foot of Schwerteck in 1855, higher up at the edge of the lateral moraines tucked tight into the cliff face at 2730m as shown on the OeAV map. This hut, comprising two small rooms and a covered terrace, lasted some 60 years before being abandoned in 1914. Developments for a new hut stalled because of the intervening war years then in 1923 the Vienna Sektion sought a more favourable site for the third hut by building on the present location, the Hasenbalfen, at a much lower level. Since 1929 when the hut was opened the hut has remained virtually unchanged apart from the addition of electricity and flushing toilets.

Not surprisingly the present four storey stone hut was built in the *gemutlichkeit* tradition of the time, complete with red and white shutters and shingle roof. The interior is equally rustic with one main dining room, several small bedrooms take up the first floor while the *matratzenlager* occupies the roof.

The present-day Salm Hut

This is a good hut in every sense of the word and if you do have time on your hands take the opportunity to search out the old huts.

Sankt Poltener Hut (2481m)

Owner	OeAV *Sektion* Polten
Location	Situated on the Falber Tauern pass that separates the Venediger from the Granat Group of mountains
Open	End of June to late September
Facilities	18B/59M Basic but adequate restaurant and toilet facilities. No hot water or showers. Good drying room.
Valley and Hut Connections	Matreier Tauern Haus 3hrs. Neue Prager Hut 7hrs. Bus service to Matrei from Tauern Haus at 10:10 and 13:10hrs.
Address	Herr Helmut Strohmaier St Poltener Huette Jesdorfer Strasse 26 A 5722 Niedersill Austria
Telephone	Hut 0043 (0) 6562 6265

Named after the small city of Sankt Poltener in the northeast of Austria, This robust three storey hut stumbled into life in the early 1900's with the planning, obtaining the site, raising funds and what have you taking from 1906 to 1912. Building work commenced in 1912 only to be halted by the First World War. Construction re-commenced in 1919 and the hut was eventually opened on 3 August 1922.

Sankt Poltener Hut and Tauern Bell in unseasonal July weather

The hut suffered badly during the Second World War when the hut was occupied by the German Army who needlessly plundered the hut's contents and generally smashed the place up.

Fortunately soon after the war once funds became available renovation work commenced albeit slowly eventually reopening in 1950. The hut was enlarged to its present size in 1980 then fully refurbished in 1992/93, when the upper floors were refurbished and the terrace added. More recently the hut went 'Green' with the installation of photo-voltaic panels and a wind turbine, which combined produce 1 kilowatt of electricity: this despite the presence of high voltage transmission pylons within a stone's throw of the front door.

The hut sits on the Falber Tauern pass, the ancient trade route linking the Venediger in the south with the Inn and Pinzgau valleys' to the north, a location that is a renowned for being windy even when the weather is calm.

Outside the hut is the famous Falber Toll bell that was used to guide travellers and those herding cows and sheep to the Tauern pass in poor weather conditions, today the bell tower is a memorial to those members who perished during two world wars.

The hut has an excellent mix of old and new particularly the alte *gaste stubl* which is much warmer than the new dining room once the fire is lit. Elsewhere are the usual hut memorabilia including chairs named after members no longer with us.

This is a fine hut in the *gemutlichkeit* tradition and is a fitting place to end the Venediger Rucksack Route and Hoehenweg.

STUDL HUT 2801M

Owner	DAV-S Oberland
Location	Situated on south side of the Fanat Scharte col that unfortunately obstructs the view of the Gross Glockner. The

views from the hut are quite extensive particularly those to the Dolomites in the south.

Open	End of June to the end of September
Facilities	104M/24N. *Matratzenlager* only, no beds. Good but limited toilet facilities due to water restrictions. Excellent menu often with buffet style evening meal and breakfast.
Valley and Hut Connections	Kals-Luckner Haus 2hrs. Adlersruhe 3hrs. Salm Hut via Pfort Scharte 2828m 3hrs.
Address	Herr Georg Oberlohr Studl Huette Koenitz 55 A-9981 Kals am Gross Glockner Austria
Telephone	Hut (0043)04876 8209 Valley 0043 (0) 4876 22144
Email	info@glocknerappartement.at
Website	www.studlhuette.at

Named after Johann Studl, a wealthy Prague businessman, who funded the construction of the hut in 1868. Studl was an active mountaineer and counted Franz Senn, founding member of the Austrian Alpine Club, and Francis Fox Tuckett, of the Alpine Club and Royal Geographical Society, among his close friends.

The hut is perhaps the main base for climbing on the Gross Glockner, particularly the normal route via the Adlersruhe climbed in 1854–55 and the more difficult Studl Grat, that bares Studl's name, which was climbed in 1864 by local guides Josef Kerer and Peter Groder. Sadly there is not much else to climb from the hut other than the Romariswandkopf (3508m) but that does not prevent the hut from being highly popular.

Opened on 15 September 1868, the hut has a long history, having been extended or refurbished in 1870, 1872 1875, 1882, 1892, 1903, 1928, 1958, 1974 and 1977. In 1992 ownership was transferred from OeAV Sektion Prague to the DAV-S Oberland and when rebuilding was discussed, the old hut was eventually demolished in 1997.

The present three storey barrel vault-shaped hut was opened in 2000 for the millennium celebrations but moreover built to replace the old hut which was gradually slipping into a state of dilapidation not for want of care but more so due to original structural building defects and the rigours of subsequent winters which

Studl Hut

allowed rain and snow to be blown in and accelerate the freeze-thaw process to the extent that the old hut was falling apart and unsafe.

Despite the somewhat radical architectural style for an alpine hut the interior is quite pleasant though functional, with lots of memorabilia from the old hut dotted about plus various signs offering words of wisdom for would be alpinists on the Gross Glockner.

SUDETENDEUTSCHE HUT (2650MM)

Owner	DAV *Sektion* Sudeten
Location	The hut is not strictly located within the Glockner Group but more correctly located within the Granat Spitze Group of mountains. Situated on a flat platform on the high alp of Viehalble overlooking the Aussere Steiner Alm valley. Excellent views toward the Grosser Muntanitz.
Open	End of June to the end of September
Facilities	23B/32M Good restaurant and toilet facilities with hot water being available at certain times of the day. Showers in the ladies toilets only.

Valley and Hut Connections	Matrei 4hrs, Rudolfs Hut 7–8hrs, Kalser Tauern Haus 4hrs.
Address	Herr Roland Rudolf Sudetendeutsche Huette Nr 170 A 6391 St Jakob Austria
Telephone	Hut 0043 (0) 4875 6466 Valley 0043 (0) 5354 56121 Mobile 0043 (0) 676 7079893
Email	rudolfroland@hotmail.com
Website	www.alpenverein-sudeten.de

Sudetendeutsche Hut

A product of the First World War, when the Austro-Hungarian Empire was carved up to the extent that between them, the Austrian and German Alpine Clubs forfeited a total of 73 huts to Italy including all those belonging to the various *Sektions* from the Sudetenland. Wanting a hut in Austria, the cost of the hut was funded by six of what remained of the 18 sections of the OeAV Sektion Sudeten after the First World War.

Built in 1929 then subsequently enlarged or refurbished in 1960, 1977 and 2003, the hut is a very traditional stone built two storey affair with painted window shutters and external sun terrace. Internally the hut has two *gaste stube* dining rooms with the usual timber panelling, with walls adorned with pictures from the old Sudetenland. That theme is carried forward to the first floor where all the bedroom doors have the heraldic coats of arms from the various provinces in the Sudetenland, Prager, Karlsbader, Silesia, Teplitzer, Aussiger and Saager. The roof is as usual dedicated to dormitory space and matratzenlager.

Venediger Haus 1691m

Owner	Private
Location	Located at Innergschloess at the dead end of the Tauerntal valley, with a commanding view of the Gross Venediger, Schwarze Wand and Schlatten-Kees glacier.
Open	Mid May to mid October
Facilities	17B/21M First class restaurant and toilet facilities as can be expected of a hotel.
Valley and Hut Connections	Taxi service to Matreier Tauern Haus then local bus service to Matrei. Neue Prager Hut 5hrs, Sankt Poltener Hut 5hrs.
Bus Service	Hohe Tauern National Park bus service operates between Matreier Tauern Haus and the bus station in Matrei Ost Tyrol. Departs Tauern Haus at 10:10 and 13:10hrs. Venediger Haus offer a minibus taxi service to/from Matreier Tauern Haus
Address	Venedigerhaus Innergschloess A-9971 Matrei in Ost Tyrol Austria
Telephone	0043 (0) 4875 8820 or 6771
Email	info@venedigerhaus-innergschloess.at
Website	www.venedigerhaus-innergschloess.at

This pleasant chalet-style two storey converted farmhouse has been providing accommodation for almost 100 years. It is situated with the last group of farms at Innergschloess which as a group of buildings provides a good visual definition of all things alpine.

Managed by the Resinger family since 1927, it is a very pleasant and friendly place to stay in the *gemutlichkeit* tradition with a nice blend of old and new with well appointed rooms and that much valued commodity for the mountain traveller, hot water.

Its strategic importance in relation to the Venediger Hohen Weg is that it can be used as a mid way point should you have poor weather while making the crossing of the Loebbentorl en route to the Neue Prager Hut and should poor weather persist it allows the Neue Prager Hut to be bypassed, with the route continuing to the Sankt Poltener Hut.

Warnsdorfer Hut (2340m)

Owner	OeAV *Sektion* Warnsdorf Krimml
Location	Situated on a rocky platform near the foot of the Gams Spitzl southwest ridge.
Open	Mid June to the end of September.
Facilities	13B/61M/12N. Good restaurant and toilet facilities with token operated showers and hot water on tap. Drying room.
Valley and Hut Connections	Krimmler Tauern Haus 2hrs. Birnlucken Hut 5hrs. Essener Rostocker Hut via Maurertorl (3108m) 5hrs. Kursinger Hut via Gamsspitzl (2888m) 8hrs.
Address	Familie Ernst and Andrea Meschik Warnsdorfer Huette Oberkrimml 30 A-5743 Krimml Austria
Telephone	Hut 0043 (0) 6564 8241 Valley 0043 (0) 6584 7676 Mobile 0043 (0) 6645 318777
Email	meschik.ernst@aon.at

This is a very good hut with a spectacular outlook, named after Warnsdorf in the Sudetenland or modern-day Czech Republic. A substantial three storey building clad with larch shingles. The hut was built in 1891, enlarged in 1926 and 1958 and then totally refurbished in 1991 to its present size as part of preparations for the hut's centenary celebrations.

The hut is very pleasant with a nice mix of old and new blended together but still maintaining that traditional rustic feel and creaking of timbers.

The new dining room adjoins the *alte gaste stubl* with walls decorated with pictures old and new – one print of particular interest is of the Krimmler Kees glacier at around 1900. Elsewhere in the *alte gaste stubl* are window panes with the crests of various towns in the Sudetenland of old Bohemia including Budweis whose name is linked to a popular beer.

There is also an impressive portrait on the dining room wall of Friedrich Ernst Berger who was the *geschaftsfuhrer* and Head of Sektion Warnsdorf many years ago and whom was instrumental in formation of the Zittauer and Neuegersdorfer Huts.

Similarly Sir Martin Conway, who stayed here in August 1894 was greatly impressed with the hospitality and made the comparison 'that you could live here

TREKKING IN AUSTRIA'S HOHE TAUERN

Warnsdorfer Hut with the Reichen Spitze above the hut's roof

for a week at less cost than you could for one night at the Grand Mulets on Mont Blanc while for accommodation there is no comparison whatsoever. That wretched Mont Blanc shelter would not be tolerated in the Tyrol'. Such a statement is probably as true today as it was in 1894.

Views from the hut are wholly dominated by the mile long ridge which leads from the Ostlicher Simony Spitz (3488m) all the way to the Drei Herrn Spitz (3497m) high above the Krimmler Kees glacier, which is truly spectacular. Elsewhere and way across the void to the northwest is the superb little Matterhorn of the region the Reichen Spitze (3303m).

ZITTAUER HUT (2329M)

Owner	OeAV *Sektion* Warnsdorf-Krimml
Location	Splendid location on the southern flank of the Reichen Spitze with attendant lake the Gerlos See, skilfully sketched and painted by the famous Victorian artist ET. Compton.
Open	Mid June to the end of September.
Facilities	7B/66M Good food and toilet facilities including hot water.
Valley and Hut Connections	Finkau-Alpe 3hrs then Gerlos 2hrs. Richter Hut via Rosskar Scharte (2690m) 4hrs. Krimmler Tauernhaus via Rainbach Scharte (2720m) 4hrs.
Address	Familie Hannes and Barbara Kogler Zittauer Huette Oberkrimml 109 A-5743 Krimml Austria
Telephone	Hut 0043 (0) 6564 8262 Valley 0043 (0) 6564 727612
Email	hanneskogler@aon.at

HUT DIRECTORY – ZITTAUER HUT

Zittauer Hut – the Reichen Spitze is the snow-covered peak on the left

This hut is in the top rank of places for the mountain traveller to stay. The hut is very friendly with a high feel-good factor of *gemutlichkeit*.

The hut is named after the Zittau in the Sudetenland in what is modern day Czech Republic. Built in 1901 then extended in 1969 and 76 then fully refurbished in 2000 to its present size in preparation for the hut's centenary celebrations.

A relatively large three-storey hut clad in larch shingles occupies a superb alpine setting adjacent to the Wildergerlos See glacial lake and appropriate mountain backdrop of the Reichen Spitze (3303m).

The dining room has the typical mix of pictures and paintings old and new including a portrait of Friedrich Ernst Berger, *geschaftsfuehrer* of the Sektion Warnsdorf, who had much influence in the area, whose portrait also adorns the walls of the Warnsdorfer Hut and whom was also instrumental in the Neugersdorfer Hut.

The main expedition from the hut is to climb the Reichen Spitze (3303m) which provides a good glacier journey with a rock scramble to finish. Aspirant alpinists may decide, once the mountain has been climbed, to press on and climb the Wildergerlos Spitze (3280m) and then descend to the Plauener Hut.

APPENDIX A
Useful Contacts

Public transport
Airlines
An internet search for flights to Munich, Innsbruck, Salzburg and Klagenfurt, using websites such as www.travelsupermarket.com, will reveal all manner of combinations that will include most, if not all, of the following airlines.
www.klm.com
www.bmibaby.com
www.austrianairlines.com
www.britishairways.com
www.thomsonfly.com
www.easyjet.com
www.ryanair.com
www.airlingus.com
www.lufthansa.com
www.flyniki.com

Railways
German Railways (DB: *Deutsche Bundesbahn*): www.reiseauskunft.bahn.de
Austrian Railways (OBB: *Osterreichische Bundesbahnen*): www.oebb.at

Buses
Post Bus: www.postbus.at

Information services
Austrian National Tourist Office
9–11 Richmond Buildings
London W1D 3HF
Tel 020 7440 3830
Holiday service tel 0845 101 1818
Fax 020 7440 3848
london@austria.info
www.austria.info
www.austriatourism.com

Austrian Alpine Club UK Section
The Manager
Austrian Alpine Club UK Section
12A North Street
Wareham
Dorset BH20 4AG
Telephone 01929 556870
Fax 01929 554729
aac.office@aac.org.uk
www.aacuk.org.uk

Austrian Alpine Club Head Office
Oesterreichischer Alpenverein
Olympia Strasse
A 6020 Innsbruck
Tel 0043 (0) 512 595
office@alpenverein.at
www.alpenverein.at

Hut Information
For a (partial) searchable directory of mountain huts, with links to emails and websites where available:
www.bergsteigen.at/de (click on 'Hütten')
www.alpenverein.at (click on 'Hütteninfos')

Mountain guiding organisations
British Association of International Mountain Leaders
www.baiml.org
in Mayrhofen:
Peter Habelers on Haupt Strasse

in Matrei in Ost Tyrol:
Guides Office on Rauterplatz
info@bf1.at
www.venediger-bergfuehrer.at

in Kals am Grossglockner:
Guides Office
info@glocknerfuehrer.at
www.glocknerfuehrer.at

APPENDIX B
German–English Glossary

English	German
When travelling	
Flughafen	Airport
Ankunft/Abflug/Abfahrt	Arrivals/departures
Hauptbahnhof	Railway station
Gleis/Bahnsteig	Platform
Auskunft	Information office
Ausgang/Eingang	Exit/entrance
Platzreservierung	Booking office
Fahrkartenschalter	Ticket office
Einfach	One way/single
Ruckfahrkarte/Hin und Zuruck	Roundtrip/return
Bushaltestelle	Bus stop
Ich moechte...	I would like...
Wo ist..?	Where is..?
Ich suche...	I'm looking for...
When eating	
Basic food and menu items	
Wiener Schnitzel	Breaded veal/pork fillets
Jager Schnitzel	Veal/pork fillets with mushroom topping

TREKKING IN AUSTRIA'S HOHE TAUERN

English	German
Tyroler Grotzl	Fried potato and eggs
Spiegeleier und Schinken	Fried eggs and bacon
Gulash	Cubes of beef in a rich sauce
Zweibelrostbraten	Broiled or fried beef with onions
Wurst Brot	Sausage and bread
Kase Brot	Cheese and bread
Schinken Brot	Ham and bread
Tagesuppe	Soup of the day
Knodelsuppe	Soup with dumplings
Wurstsuppe	Soup with sausages
Kaiserschmarren	Sweet pancakes
Apfelstrudel	Apple pie
Compote	Fresh or tinned fruit
Bergsteigeressen	Pot luck climber's meal at low cost
Brot/Brotchen	Bread/Bread rolls
Kartoffeln	Potato
Gemuse	Vegetables
Reis	Rice
Salt	Salt
Pfeffer	Pepper
Senf	Mustard

Vegetarian options

Kasspatzle	Cheese with noodles
Kartoffel-gaertreide-bratlinge mit salat garniture	Pan fried potatoes with salad garnish
Kartoffel mit spiegeleier	Pan fried potatoes with fried egg
Gemischter salat	Mixed salad
Gruner salat	Green salad

Drinks

Bier	Beer
Weiss/Rot Wein	White/Red Wine
Schnapps	Clear strong alcoholic spirit aka rocket fuel!
Tee/Café/Milch	Tea/Coffee/Milk
Zitronen	Lemonade

APPENDIX B – GERMAN–ENGLISH GLOSSARY

English	German
Heiss/Kalt	Hot/Cold
Gross/Klein	Large/Small
Viertel/Halb	Quarter/Half

Other useful food-related words

Speisekarte	Menu
Tasse	Cup
Teller	Plate
Schussel	Bowl
Messer	Knife
Gabel	Fork
Loffel	Spoon

When ordering or paying

Wie bitte	Excuse me
Sprechen Sie Englisch?	Do you speak English?
Wieviel? or Mein Zahlen bitte?	How much? or My bill, please.
Die Rechnung bitte	The bill please
Kann ich habe…?	Can I have…?
Haben sie…?	Have you…?
Haben sie vegetarische Gerichte Essen?	Have you any vegetarian meals?

APPENDIX C
Further Reading

Hut Directory

Alpenvereinshutten: Volume 1 Ostalpen: Deutschland, Oesterreich, Sudtyrol OeAV, AVS and DAV Bergverlag Rother (2005)

A comprehensive listing of all the mountain huts in the Eastern Alps, with contact information, opening hours, GPS coordinates and much more.

Guide Books

Dieter Seibert *Eastern Alps: The Classic Routes of the Highest Peaks* Diadem Books (1992)

Includes the Reichen Spitze, Wildgerloz Spitze, Gross Glockner, Gross Venediger, Grosses Weisbachhorn, Drei Herrn Spitz, Granat Spitze, Stubacher Sonnblick and Ost Simony Spitz.

Hubert Peterka *Kleiner Führer durch die Glockner-, Granatspitz- und Venediger-Gruppe (Compact Guide)* Bergverlag Rother (1980)

Inspirational reading

Readers may find the following mountaineering books from mountain lovers long ago interesting and inspiring – if you can track them down!

Sir Martin Conway *The Alps from End to End* Archibald Constable & Co (1895)

Frank Smythe *Over Tyrolese Hills* Hodder and Stoughton (1936)

Francis Fox Tuckett *Pictures in Tyrol and Elsewhere* Longmans, Green & Co (1867)

APPENDIX D
Across the Hohe Tauern National Park

As mentioned at the start of this guidebook it is possible to traverse the entire National Park within the space of a two week holiday. This particular itinerary is more suited to aspirant alpinists as the journey includes several glacier crossings.

Suggested Itinerary
The route starts in the Reichen Group, passes through the Venediger and after crossing the Gross Glockner ends at Glockner Haus.

	Standard Time (hrs)	Distance (km)	Ascent (m)
Reichen Group			
Day 1 Innsbruck to Mayrhofen to Plauener Hut Follow approach notes and route description as Stage 1.	2	3	500
Day 2 At Plauener Hut Excursion from Plauener Hut: 1.1 Ascent of the Reichen Spitze	4–5	3+	930
Day 3 Plauener Hut to Birnlucken Hut/ Richter Hut Follow route description as Stage 2. *or* Reverse route description as Stage 7A to Richter Hut	7 7	12 9	1000+ 800
Day 4 Richter Hut/Birnlucken Hut to Warnsdorfer Hut. Follow route description as Stage 3. *or* From Richter Hut walk down the valley east to Krimmler Tauern Haus (see map on p64), and then follow route description as Stage 1 on the Venediger Glacier Tour.	4 5	5 12	600 700
Venediger Group			
Day 5 Warnsdorfer Hut to Kursinger Hut Reverse route description for Stage 8 on the Venediger Glacier Tour.	8	7+	1000+

TREKKING IN AUSTRIA'S HOHE TAUERN

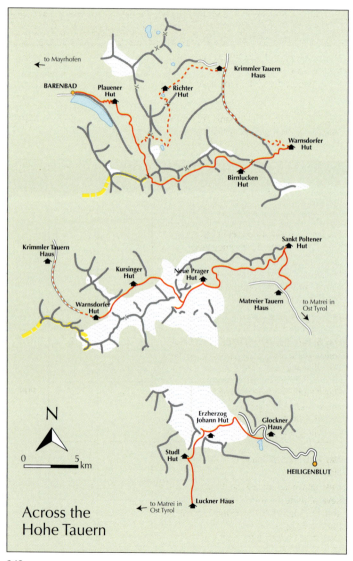

Across the Hohe Tauern

Appendix D – Across the Hohe Tauern National Park

	Standard Time (hrs)	Distance (km)	Ascent (m)
Day 6 Kursinger Hut to Neue Prager Hut via the Gross Venediger Reverse route description for Stage 7 on the Venediger Glacier Tour.	7+	10	900
Day 7 Neue Prager Hut to Sankt Poltener Hut Follow route description as Stage 6 on the Venediger Rucksack Route.	7	14+	600+
Day 8, Part 1 Sankt Poltener Hut to Luckner Haus Follow route description as Stage 7 on the Venediger Rucksack Route to Matreier Tauern Haus. Local bus service to Matrei in Ost Tyrol (dep 10:10 and 13:10, journey time 20–30mins). Local bus service to Luckner Haus via Huben (dep 14:19, arrives 15:24, change at Huben).	3 + bus	6 + bus	nil
Gross Glockner Group			
Day 8, Part 2 Luckner Haus to Studl Hut Follow route description as Stage 1 of the Glockner Rucksack Route.	2.5	4	820
Day 9 Studl Hut to Erzherzog Johann Hut Follow route description as Excursions from the Studl Hut: 1.1 Ascent of the Gross Glockner on the Glockner Rucksack Route.	5	2.5	900
Day 10 Erzherzog Johann Hut to Glockner Haus Descent via the Meletzkigrat ridge. Reverse route description as Excursions from the Studl Hut: 1.2 on the Glockner Rucksack Route.	8	9	200+

INDEX

A
Adlersruhe 135,138,140,143,145,147
. . . . 152-153,199-200
Ahrntal. 53,57-59,69-70
Alfred Kaindl 170
Alpenverein 23,50,212
Alpenvereinskarte (Maps) 32,47,79,119,135
Alte Prager Hut. 94,96-7,101,219
Amertal 75,129
Anton Franz Richter 220-221
Archduke Johann 153,200,208-9
Archduke Rudolf 222-3
Aussergschloss 103
Austrian Alpine Club (OeAV) 2,20-21,23,26,28,132,181,193,236

B
Baden. 96
Badener Hut. 78,88,94,97,99,105,116,194
Bahnhof 14
Barenbad 43,47
Beim Seewl 56
Bergfuehrer. 24,41,188
Bergrettung. 22,29
Birnlucke 45,59
Birnlucken Hut. 23,46,53,57-9,70,111,195
Blauewand 138
Blaueswandl. 137
Bonn Matreier Hut 78,85,87-9,91-2,105,116,196
Brandl Scharte 167,171

C
Crevasse Rescue. 34-7

D
Dachstein. 162,164
Defregger Haus 197
Dolomites. 143
Dorfertal. 149,181,184,188

INDEX

Dorfer See 189-190
Drei Herrn Spitz 53,57,59,61-2,70,72,75,83,87
. . . . 107-8,111,115,119,124,127

E
Eastern Alps 11,34,75,129,145,155
Eiskogele 181
Eissee 67,69,87,104
Eissee Hut 78,85,88,115,198
Emergency Telephone Numbers 7,22,29
Erdiges Eck 185,189
Erzherzog Johann Adlersruhe Hut 135,138,143-4,199-200
Essener Rostocker Hut 78,82,105,107,110,115-6,201-2

F
Falber Tauern 103
Fanat Scharte 138,140,151
Ferleiten 158-9
Fochez Kees 169
Franz Josef Haus 129,143,145-7,154-5
Frosnitz Kees 92
Frosnitztal 89,91,94
Fruschnitz Kees 35,92,148-150
Fusch 132,134,155,159-162,202
Fuschertal 129,156-7,159

G
Galten Scharte 88-9,91-2,99
Gams Scharte 50,71,73
Gams Spitzl 107-8,122,124,126-7
Gasthof Wasserfall 159,161,202
Geistjochl 53,56,58,70
Gemutlichkeit 26,190,204,206,211-2,219,221,225,227,231,233
German words/phrases 28-9,31,237-239
Gerlos See 62,233
Gesprutt 98,125,138
Gleiwitzer Hut 132,134,159,161-2,167,171,203
Gleiwitzer Hoehen Weg 164
Glockner Haus 132,134,143-4,147,153-6

Glockner Runde Tour 12,132,160,162,171,181,186-7,189
Glockner Scharte 140-1,143-4
Glorer Hut 137,152,205
Gradetz Sattel. 181,186
Gradetz Kees 186-8
Granat Scharte 176-9,184
Granat Spitze 149,169,172,174-181,188
Granat Spitze Group. 75,78-9,89,101,129,149,188
Gross Geiger 75,87,108,110-2,115,119,121,124-5
Gross Glockner 11-2,21,26,34,79,119,129,132,135,138
. . . . 140-1,144-5,147-8,151-2,156,169,181,188
Gross Glockner Group 75,78,128-9,132,134,168-9
Grosser Muntanitz 89,149,181,187-8
Gross Venediger .11,21,26,34,61,72,75,84,89,94,96,101
. . . . 115-6,119-20,124,143,148-9,169,188,191
Grosses Weisbachhorn 119,134,143,149,162,164,166,168,170,176
Gruben. 99

H
Hapsburg 119
Hauptbahnhof 13-4
Heinrich Schwaiger Haus 132,134,162,166-8,171-2,206
Heiligenblut 129
Hinterbichl 80
Hirzbachtal 161-2,164
Hofmanns Kees 140,145-6
Hofmanns Hut 143,145-6,155,207-8
Hohe Riffl. 149,153,164,175
Hohe Tauern. 34
Hohe Tauern National Park. 9,11-2,26,43,75,78,104,129,132,241
Hoher Zaun 94
Hotels. 15-6
Huben 135
Huttenwirt 24
Hut Directory 23,26,192,240

I
In der Au 43
Inn 43,75
Innsbruck 12-18,106,134-5,191

Innergschloss 102
Italy 23,43,54,56,58-9,69

J
Jager Scharte.. 164,167
Jenbach 13,106
Johannisberg......................................143,147,149,153
Johannis Hut........................... 78,82,85,105,111,116,208-9
Johann Studl.................................... 208,220,228
Johann Studl Weg..................................... 151

K
Kaindlgrat.. 169-170
Kaiserin Elisabeth (Sisi)................................ 222
Kalber Scharte.. 89-90
Kals 11,134-5,181,186
Kalser Tauern.................................... 185-6,188-9
Kalser Tauern Haus............... 132,134,176,181,185-6,188-190,210-1
Kaprun 15,129,134,167,171,181
Kaprunertorl.................................. 166,172,174-5
Keesboden... 97-8
Keeskogel... 121-2
Kesselfall Alpenhaus................................... 167
Kempsenkopf.. 164,166
Kit 33,39,41
Kitzbuhel.. 11,14-5,75,80,134-5,191
Klein Glockner....................................... 141,144
Kleiner Muntanitz..................................... 187,189
Klettersteig.. 63,84,140
Koednitz Kees.. 140
Koednitztal.. 151
Krimml 43,106-7
Krimmler Achental 43,61-2,75,107
Krimler Kees.. 59,61,107
Krimmler Tauern.................................... 57,69,211-2
Krimmler Tauern Haus 46,61-3,106-7,211-2
Krimmler Runde Tour,................................ 46
Kuchelmoos Kees.................................... 50,71-2
Kursinger 213-4
Kursinger Hut........................ 78,105,116,119,120-2,125,212-4

L

Landgasthof Wasserfall	159,161,202
Leitertal	154
Loebbentorl	12,94,96-7,99
Luckner Haus	134-5,152,215
Luckner Hut	135,137,215
Luisengrat	140,148

M

Mannlkarb	66
Maps	9,18,32-3,44-5,47,76,79,130,134
Matrei in Ost Tyrol	11,15-8,75,80,96,134-5,181,190-1
Matrei Tauern Haus	78,93,104
Maurer Kees	110
Maurertal	82
Maurertorl	107-8,125
Mayrhofen	12-3,15-6,18,43,47,106
Meletzkigrat	143-6
Mittersill	11,134,181
Mountain Guides	41,236
Munchen Ost	14

N

Neugersdorfer Hut	57-8
Neue Prager Hut	78,93-4,96-7,99,101,105,116,118,220
Neue Further Hut	102
Neue Thuringer Hut	102

O

Obersulzbach Kees	30,35,108,119-126
Oberwalder Hut	143,155,216
Oetztal Wild Spitze	119

P

Pasterzen Kees	34,129,145-7,153-5
Paths	29-30
Pfandl Scharte	156,158,160
Pfandl Scharten Kees	157-8,160
Pfaffenschneide	55
Pfort Scharte	151-2

Pinzgau 11,75,129,135,181
Plauener Hut 13,46-7,52-3,56,67,70,72-3,218
Post Office 19
Pragraten 17,75,87

R
Rainbach Scharte 12,62-3,65
Rainbach See 62-3
Rainbachkeeskar 67
Rainerhorn 84,94,119
Rauchkofel 53,56,70
Reichen Group 11-3,42,46,67,69,75
Reichen Group Runde Tour 30,46,70
Reichen Spitze 43,49,52,62-3,65,115,119
Richter Hut 43,46,52-3,56,62,65-6,67,69,71-3,222
Romariswandkopf 35,148-9,181,185,188
Rosskar 66
Rosskarlaeke 66
Rosskar Scharte 65-6
Rudolfs Hut Berg Hotel 132,134,149,166-7,172,174-5,
. . . . 179-181,184,189-190,223
Rotes Kreuz 22,29

S
Sajat Hut 85,225
Salm Hut 132,134,137,144,151-3,155,226
Salzburg 11,14,16,134
Sankt Poltener Hut 78,93,99,101,227
Sankt Poltener Hoehen Weg 75,78,103-4,184
Saulkopf 89
Schere 148
Schlaten Kees 94,96,116,119,121
Schwarze Wand 94,96,101,116,119
Schwerteck 152-4
Seebach 189
Seewande 176,180
Sektion Britannia 2,21,23
Silesia Hoehen Weg 181,185
Simony Spitz 87,109,112,114-5,119,124,127,143
Simony Kees 113,115

Sonnblick Kees 176-7,179-180
Sonnblick Scharte. 177
Sonntaglahnerkopf 48
South Tyrol 43
Spitzbrett 164
Steiner Alm. 190
Streden. 79,82
Stocker Scharte. 154-5
Stubacher Sonnblick. 149,169,172,175,178,181,188
Studl Hut 132-3,135,140,143,151,228
Studlgrat. 148
Stausee Margaritzen. 147,154
Stausee Mooserboden. 164,166-8,172
Sudetendeutsche Hut 132,134,176,181,186-7
. 189,190-1,230

T
Tauerntal 75,101,103,129,190
Taurschneide 55,57
Teischnitz Kees. 148
Tennen Gebirge 162
Teufelkamp. 148-9
Teufelmuel Kees 170
Tyrol. 11,17,34
Tourist information 18-9,159
Travel information 14-5,47,80,99,106,134-5,168,191,214,235
Turmljoch. 82,84,87,112

U
Umbal Kees 35,111
Uttendorf 129,181

V
Venediger. 12,43,67,69,75,78,94,96,129,143,176
Venedig 14
Venediger Group 11,52,74-5,79,105
Venediger Haus 93,99,101-2,232
Venediger Hoehen Weg 30,75,78,85-6,93-4,99,101,103-4
Venediger Scharte. 108,119,120-1
Via ferrata. 63,140

Virgen 75,181
Virgental. 11,17,75,78,87,191

W
Warnsdorfer Hut. 46,52,61-3,72,78,105-6,115,122,233
Weissee 149,176,179-181,184
Weilinger Kees 170
Wiener Hohen Weg 154
Wild Park 156,159
Wildergerlos Spitze 43,52,71-2
Wilo Walzenbach. 170
Windbach Scharte 67,70
Windbachtal. 67,69

Z
Zell am See 11,13-5,129,164,181
Zillergrundl 43,47,53,56
Zillertal. 16,43,58,67,69,75
Ziller Platten Scharte 56,67,70
Zittauer Hut 46,52,62,65,234
Zopat Scharte 12,85,87-8

The UK's leading monthly magazine for the independent hilllwalker and backpacker. With thought provoking articles, varied and exhilarating routes, expert gear reviews and outstanding photography, TGO's writers are at the heart of the walking world providing the essentials to inspire your next adventure.

To subscribe today call

0141 302 7718

Get ready for take off

Adventure Travel helps you to go outdoors, over there.

More ideas, information, advice and entertaining features on overseas trekking, walking and backpacking than any other magazine – guaranteed.

Available from good newsagents or by subscription – 6 issues £15.

Adventure Travel Magazine T: 01789 488166.

LISTING OF CICERONE GUIDES

BRITISH ISLES CHALLENGES, COLLECTIONS AND ACTIVITIES
The Mountains of England and Wales
  Vol 1 Wales
  Vol 2 England
The UK Trailwalker's Handbook
The Ridges of England, Wales and Ireland
The End to End Trail
The National Trails
Three Peaks, Ten Tors
The Relative Hills of Britain

NORTHERN ENGLAND TRAILS
The Pennine Way
The Spirit of Hadrian's Wall
A Northern Coast to Coast Walk
The Dales Way
Hadrian's Wall Path
The Pennine Way
Backpacker's Britain: Northern England

LAKE DISTRICT
The Mid-Western Fells
The Southern Fells
The Near Eastern Fells
The Central Fells
Great Mountain Days in the Lake District
Tour of the Lake District
Lake District Winter Climbs
Scrambles in the Lake District
  North
  South
The Cumbria Coastal Way
An Atlas of the English Lakes
Rocky Rambler's Wild Walks
Short Walks in Lakeland
  Book 1: South Lakeland
  Book 2: North Lakeland
  Book 3: West Lakeland
The Lake District Anglers' Guide
Roads and Tracks of the Lake District
The Cumbria Way and the Allerdale Ramble
The Tarns of Lakeland
  Vol 1: West
  Vol 2: East
Walks in Silverdale and Arnside
Coniston Copper Mines

NORTH WEST ENGLAND AND THE ISLE OF MAN
Walking on the West Pennine Moors
Walking in the Forest of Bowland and Pendle
The Ribble Way
Walks in Lancashire Witch Country
Walking in Lancashire
Isle of Man Coastal Path
The Isle of Man
Historic Walks in Cheshire
Walks in Ribble Country
Walks in The Forest of Bowland
A Walker's Guide to the Lancaster Canal

NORTH EAST ENGLAND, YORKSHIRE DALES AND PENNINES
Walking in County Durham
The Reivers Way
Walking in the North Pennines
The Yorkshire Dales
  North and East
  South and West
Walks in the Yorkshire Dales
The Teesdale Way
The North York Moors
The Cleveland Way and the Yorkshire Wolds Way
Walking in Northumberland
South Pennine Walks
Historic Walks in North Yorkshire
Walks in Dales Country
The Yorkshire Dales Angler's Guide
Walks on the North York Moors
  Books 1 & 2
Walking in the Wolds
A Canoeist's Guide to the North East

DERBYSHIRE, PEAK DISTRICT AND MIDLANDS
White Peak Walks
  The Northern Dales
  The Southern Dales
Historic Walks in Derbyshire
The Star Family Walks
High Peak Walks

SOUTHERN ENGLAND
Walking in the Isles of Scilly
Walking in the Thames Valley
The Cotswold Way
The Lea Valley Walk
Walking in Kent
The Thames Path
The South Downs Way
Walking in Sussex
The South West Coast Path
Walking on Dartmoor
The Greater Ridgeway
London: The Definitive Walking Guide
Walking in Berkshire
The North Downs Way
Walking in Bedfordshire
Walking in Buckinghamshire
A Walker's Guide to the Isle of Wight

WALES AND WELSH BORDERS
Great Mountain Days in Snowdonia
Walking on the Brecon Beacons
Offa's Dyke Path
The Lleyn Peninsula Coastal Path
Hillwalking in Wales
  Vols 1 & 2
Walking in Pembrokeshire
The Shropshire Hills
Backpacker's Britain: Wales
The Pembrokeshire Coastal Path
Ridges of Snowdonia
Hillwalking in Snowdonia
Glyndwr's Way

The Spirit Paths of Wales
Scrambles in Snowdonia
The Ascent of Snowdon
Welsh Winter Climbs

SCOTLAND
Walking on the Orkney and Shetland Isles
Walking on Harris and Lewis
The Isle of Skye
Walking Loch Lomond and the Trossachs
Backpacker's Britain: Central and Southern Scottish Highlands
The Great Glen Way
Ben Nevis and Glen Coe
The Pentland Hills: A Walker's Guide
Walking on the Isle of Arran
Scotland's Mountain Ridges
Walking in Torridon
The Border Country
Backpacker's Britain: Northern Scotland
Walking in the Ochils, Campsie Fells and Lomond Hills
Walking in the Cairngorms
The Southern Upland Way
Scotland's Far West
Walking the Munros
  Vol 1: Southern, Central and Western Highlands
  Vol 2: Northern Highlands and the Cairngorms
Walking in Scotland's Far North
The West Highland Way
Winter Climbs: Ben Nevis and Glencoe
Winter Climbs in the Cairngorms
North to the Cape
Walking the Lowther Hills
The Central Highlands
Walking in the Hebrides
The Scottish Glens
  2: The Atholl Glens
  3: The Glens of Rannoch
  4: The Glens of Trossach
  5: The Glens of Argyll
  6: The Great Glen
Scrambles in Lochaber
Border Pubs and Inns
Walking the Galloway Hills

UK CYCLING
The Lancashire Cycleway
Border Country Cycle Routes
South Lakeland Cycle Rides
Rural Rides No 2: East Surrey
Lands End to John O'Groats Cycle Guide

ALPS: CROSS BORDER ROUTES
Walks and Treks in the Maritime Alps
Tour of Mont Blanc
Chamonix to Zermatt

Across the Eastern Alps: E5
Walking in the Alps
Tour of the Matterhorn
100 Hut Walks in the Alps
Alpine Points of View
Tour of Monte Rosa
Snowshoeing
Alpine Ski Mountaineering
  Vol 1: Western Alps
  Vol 2: Central and Eastern Alps
FRANCE
Mont Blanc Walks
Tour of the Vanoise
Tour of the Oisans: The GR54
The GR5 Trail
Walking in the Languedoc
Écrins National Park
The Robert Louis Stevenson Trail
Tour of the Queyras
The Cathar Way
GR20: Corsica
Trekking in the Vosges and Jura
Walking in the Cathar Region
Walking in the Dordogne
Mont Blanc Walks
Walking in the Haute Savoie
  North
  South
Walking on Corsica
Walking in Provence
Vanoise Ski Touring
Walking in the Cevennes
Walking in the Tarentaise & Beaufortain Alps
Walking the French Gorges
Walks in Volcano Country
PYRENEES AND FRANCE/SPAIN CROSS-BORDER ROUTES
The Pyrenean Haute Route
Through the Spanish Pyrenees: GR11
Walks and Climbs in the Pyrenees
The Mountains of Andorra
Way of St James
  France
  Spain
The GR10 Trail
Rock Climbs In The Pyrenees
SPAIN & PORTUGAL
Walking in Madeira
Walking the GR7 in Andalucia
Trekking through Mallorca
Walking in Mallorca
Via de la Plata
Walking in the Algarve
Walking in the Sierra Nevada
Walking in the Canary Islands
  Vol 2 East
Walking in the Cordillera Cantabrica
Costa Blanca Walks
  Vol 1 West
  Vol 2 East
The Mountains of Central Spain
Walks and Climbs in the Picos de Europa
SWITZERLAND
Tour of the Jungfrau Region
The Bernese Alps

Walks in the Engadine
Alpine Pass Route
Walking in the Valais
Walking in Ticino
GERMANY
Walking in the Bavarian Alps
Walking the River Rhine Trail
Germany's Romantic Road
Walking in the Harz Mountains
Walking in the Salzkammergut
King Ludwig Way
EASTERN EUROPE
Walking in Bulgaria's National Parks
The High Tatras
Walking in Hungary
The Mountains of Romania
SCANDINAVIA
Walking in Norway
SLOVENIA, CROATIA AND MONTENEGRO
Trekking in Slovenia
The Mountains of Montenegro
The Julian Alps of Slovenia
ITALY
Via Ferratas of the Italian Dolomites
  Vols 1 & 2
Italy's Sibillini National Park
Gran Paradiso
Walking in Tuscany
Through the Italian Alps
Trekking in the Apennines
Walking in Sicily
Walking in the Dolomites
Treks in the Dolomites
Shorter Walks in the Dolomites
Central Apennines of Italy
Walking in the Central Italian Alps
Italian Rock
MEDITERRANEAN
The High Mountains of Crete
Jordan: Walks, Treks, Caves, Climbs and Canyons
The Mountains of Greece
Walking in Malta
Western Crete
Treks & Climbs in Wadi Rum, Jordan
The Ala Dag
HIMALAYA
Bhutan
The Mount Kailash Trek
Everest: A Trekker's Guide
Annapurna: A Trekker's Guide
Manaslu: A Trekker's Guide
Kangchenjunga: A Trekker's Guide
Garhwal & Kumaon: A Trekker's and Visitor's Guide
Langtang with Gosainkund & Helambu: A Trekker's Guide
NORTH AMERICA
The Grand Canyon
British Columbia
SOUTH AMERICA
Aconcagua and the Southern Andes
AFRICA
Walking in the Drakensberg
Trekking in the Atlas Mountains

Kilimanjaro: A Complete Trekker's Guide
Climbing in the Moroccan Anti-Atlas
IRELAND
The Irish Coast To Coast Walk
Irish Coastal Walks
The Mountains Of Ireland
EUROPEAN CYCLING
The Grand Traverse of the Massif Central
Cycle Touring in Ireland
Cycling the Canal du Midi
Cycling in the French Alps
Cycle Touring in Switzerland
The Way of St James
Cycle Touring in France
Cycling the River Loire
Cycle Touring in Spain
The Danube Cycleway
INTERNATIONAL CHALLENGES, COLLECTIONS AND ACTIVITIES
Europe's High Points
Canyoning
AUSTRIA
Trekking in Austria's Hohe Tauern
Walking in Austria
Trekking in the Zillertal Alps
Trekking in the Stubai Alps
Klettersteig: Scrambles in the Northern Limestone Alps
TECHNIQUES
Indoor Climbing
The Book of the Bivvy
Moveable Feasts
Rock Climbing
Sport Climbing
Mountain Weather
Map and Compass
The Hillwalker's Guide to Mountaineering
Outdoor Photography
The Hillwalker's Manual
Beyond Adventure
Snow and Ice Techniques
MINI GUIDES
Pocket First Aid and Wilderness Medicine
Navigating with a GPS
Navigation
Snow
Avalanche!

For full and up-to-date information on our ever-expanding list of guides, please visit our website:
www.cicerone.co.uk.

Cicerone's mission is to inform and inspire by providing the best guides to exploring the world

Since its foundation 40 years ago, Cicerone has specialised in publishing guidebooks and has built a reputation for quality and reliability. It now publishes nearly 300 guides to the major destinations for outdoor enthusiasts, including Europe, UK and the rest of the world.

Written by leading and committed specialists, Cicerone guides are recognised as the most authoritative. They are full of information, maps and illustrations so that the user can plan and complete a successful and safe trip or expedition – be it a long face climb, a walk over Lakeland fells, an alpine cycling tour, a Himalayan trek or a ramble in the countryside.

With a thorough introduction to assist planning, clear diagrams, maps and colour photographs to illustrate the terrain and route, and accurate and detailed text, Cicerone guides are designed for ease of use and access to the information.

If the facts on the ground change, or there is any aspect of a guide that you think we can improve, we are always delighted to hear from you.

Cicerone Press
2 Police Square Milnthorpe Cumbria LA7 7PY
Tel: 015395 62069 Fax: 015395 63417
info@cicerone.co.uk www.cicerone.co.uk